GOSPEL OF MATTHEW

TODAY'S NEW
INTERNATIONAL VERSION

Hodder & Stoughton
LONDON SYDNEY AUCKLAND

Matthew

The genealogy of Jesus the Messiah

1 This is the genealogy[a] of Jesus the Messiah[b] the son of David, the son of Abraham:

²Abraham was the father of Isaac,
   Isaac the father of Jacob,
   Jacob the father of Judah and his brothers,
   ³Judah the father of Perez and Zerah, whose mother was
      Tamar,
   Perez the father of Hezron,
   Hezron the father of Ram,
   ⁴Ram the father of Amminadab,
   Amminadab the father of Nahshon,
   Nahshon the father of Salmon,
   ⁵Salmon the father of Boaz, whose mother was Rahab,
   Boaz the father of Obed, whose mother was Ruth,
   Obed the father of Jesse,
   ⁶and Jesse the father of King David.

---

a 1 Or *is an account of the origin*
b 1 Or *Jesus Christ.* "Messiah" (Hebrew) and "Christ" (Greek) both mean "Anointed One";
also in verse 18.

David was the father of Solomon, whose mother had been
  Uriah's wife,
[7]Solomon the father of Rehoboam,
  Rehoboam the father of Abijah,
  Abijah the father of Asa,
  [8]Asa the father of Jehoshaphat,
  Jehoshaphat the father of Jehoram,
  Jehoram the father of Uzziah,
  [9]Uzziah the father of Jotham,
  Jotham the father of Ahaz,
  Ahaz the father of Hezekiah,
[10]Hezekiah the father of Manasseh,
  Manasseh the father of Amon,
  Amon the father of Josiah,
[11]and Josiah the father of Jeconiah[c] and his brothers at the
  time of the exile to Babylon.

[12]After the exile to Babylon:
  Jeconiah was the father of Shealtiel,
  Shealtiel the father of Zerubbabel,
  [13]Zerubbabel the father of Abiud,
  Abiud the father of Eliakim,
  Eliakim the father of Azor,
  [14]Azor the father of Zadok,
  Zadok the father of Akim,
  Akim the father of Eliud,
  [15]Eliud the father of Eleazar,
  Eleazar the father of Matthan,
  Matthan the father of Jacob,

---

c 11 That is, Jehoiachin; also in verse 12

[16]and Jacob the father of Joseph, the husband of Mary, and Mary was the mother of Jesus who is called the Messiah.

[17]Thus there were fourteen generations in all from Abraham to David, fourteen from David to the exile to Babylon, and fourteen from the exile to the Messiah.

Joseph accepts Jesus as his son

[18]This is how the birth of Jesus the Messiah came about[d]: His mother Mary was pledged to be married to Joseph, but before they came together, she was found to be pregnant through the Holy Spirit. [19]Because Joseph her husband was a righteous man and did not want to expose her to public disgrace, he had in mind to divorce her quietly.

[20]But after he had considered this, an angel of the Lord appeared to him in a dream and said, "Joseph son of David, do not be afraid to take Mary home as your wife, because what is conceived in her is from the Holy Spirit. [21]She will give birth to a son, and you are to give him the name Jesus,[e] because he will save his people from their sins."

[22]All this took place to fulfil what the Lord had said through the prophet: [23]"The virgin will conceive and give birth to a son, and they will call him Immanuel"[f]—which means, "God with us."

[24]When Joseph woke up, he did what the angel of the Lord had commanded him and took Mary home as his wife. [25]But he had no union with her until she gave birth to a son. And he gave him the name Jesus.

---

d 18 Or *The origin of Jesus the Messiah was like this*
e 21 *Jesus* is the Greek form of *Joshua*, which means *the LORD saves.*
f 23 Isaiah 7:14

The Magi visit the Messiah

2 After Jesus was born in Bethlehem in Judea, during the time of King Herod, Magi[a] from the east came to Jerusalem ²and asked, "Where is the one who has been born king of the Jews? We saw his star when it rose and have come to worship him."

³When King Herod heard this he was disturbed, and all Jerusalem with him. ⁴When he had called together all the people's chief priests and teachers of the law, he asked them where the Messiah was to be born. ⁵"In Bethlehem in Judea," they replied, "for this is what the prophet has written:

⁶" 'But you, Bethlehem, in the land of Judah,
   are by no means least among the rulers of Judah;
 for out of you will come a ruler
   who will shepherd my people Israel.'[b] "

⁷Then Herod called the Magi secretly and found out from them the exact time the star had appeared. ⁸He sent them to Bethlehem and said, "Go and make a careful search for the child. As soon as you find him, report to me, so that I too may go and worship him."

⁹After they had heard the king, they went on their way, and the star they had seen when it rose went ahead of them until it stopped over the place where the child was. ¹⁰When they saw the star, they were overjoyed. ¹¹On coming to the house, they saw the child with his mother Mary, and they bowed down and worshipped him. Then they opened their treasures and

a 1 Traditionally *wise men*
b 6 Micah 5:2,4

presented him with gifts of gold, frankincense and myrrh.
[12]And having been warned in a dream not to go back to Herod,
they returned to their country by another route.

The escape to Egypt

[13]When they had gone, an angel of the Lord appeared to
Joseph in a dream. "Get up," he said, "take the child and his
mother and escape to Egypt. Stay there until I tell you, for
Herod is going to search for the child to kill him."

[14]So he got up, took the child and his mother during the
night and left for Egypt, [15]where he stayed until the death of
Herod. And so was fulfilled what the Lord had said through
the prophet: "Out of Egypt I called my son."[c]

[16]When Herod realised that he had been outwitted by the
Magi, he was furious, and he gave orders to kill all the boys in
Bethlehem and its vicinity who were two years old and under,
in accordance with the time he had learned from the Magi.
[17]Then what was said through the prophet Jeremiah was
fulfilled:

[18]"A voice is heard in Ramah,
    weeping and great mourning,
Rachel weeping for her children
    and refusing to be comforted,
because they are no more."[d]

The return to Nazareth

[19]After Herod died, an angel of the Lord appeared in a dream
to Joseph in Egypt [20]and said, "Get up, take the child and his

---

c 15 Hosea 11:1
d 18 Jer. 31:15

mother and go to the land of Israel, for those who were trying to take the child's life are dead."

[21]So he got up, took the child and his mother and went to the land of Israel. [22]But when he heard that Archelaus was reigning in Judea in place of his father Herod, he was afraid to go there. Having been warned in a dream, he withdrew to the district of Galilee, [23]and he went and lived in a town called Nazareth. So was fulfilled what was said through the prophets: "He will be called a Nazarene."

John the Baptist prepares the way

3 In those days John the Baptist came, preaching in the wilderness of Judea [2]and saying, "Repent, for the kingdom of heaven has come near." [3]This is he who was spoken of through the prophet Isaiah:

"A voice of one calling in the wilderness,
'Prepare the way for the Lord,
　　make straight paths for him.' "[a]

[4]John's clothes were made of camel's hair, and he had a leather belt round his waist. His food was locusts and wild honey. [5]People went out to him from Jerusalem and all Judea and the whole region of the Jordan. [6]Confessing their sins, they were baptised by him in the River Jordan.

[7]But when he saw many of the Pharisees and Sadducees coming to where he was baptising, he said to them: "You brood of vipers! Who warned you to flee from the coming wrath? [8]Produce fruit in keeping with repentance. [9]And do not think you can say to yourselves, 'We have Abraham as our

---

a 3 Isaiah 40:3

father.' I tell you that out of these stones God can raise up children for Abraham. [10]The axe has been laid to the root of the trees, and every tree that does not produce good fruit will be cut down and thrown into the fire.

[11]"I baptise you with[b] water for repentance. But after me comes one who is more powerful than I, whose sandals I am not worthy to carry. He will baptise you with[b] the Holy Spirit and fire. [12]His winnowing fork is in his hand, and he will clear his threshing-floor, gathering his wheat into the barn and burning up the chaff with unquenchable fire."

The baptism of Jesus

[13]Then Jesus came from Galilee to the Jordan to be baptised by John. [14]But John tried to deter him, saying, "I need to be baptised by you, and do you come to me?"

[15]Jesus replied, "Let it be so now; it is proper for us to do this to fulfil all righteousness." Then John consented.

[16]As soon as Jesus was baptised, he went up out of the water. At that moment heaven was opened, and he saw the Spirit of God descending like a dove and alighting on him. [17]And a voice from heaven said, "This is my Son, whom I love; with him I am well pleased."

Jesus is tested in the wilderness

4 Then Jesus was led by the Spirit into the wilderness to be tempted[a] by the devil. [2]After fasting for forty days and forty nights, he was hungry. [3]The tempter came to him and said, "If you are the Son of God, tell these stones to become bread."

---

b 11 Or *in*
a 1 The Greek for *tempted* can also mean *tested*.

[4]Jesus answered, "It is written: 'People do not live on bread alone, but on every word that comes from the mouth of God.'[b] "

[5]Then the devil took him to the holy city and set him on the highest point of the temple. [6]"If you are the Son of God," he said, "throw yourself down. For it is written:

" 'He will command his angels concerning you,
   and they will lift you up in their hands,
so that you will not strike your foot against a stone.'[c] "

[7]Jesus answered him, "It is also written: 'Do not put the Lord your God to the test.'[d] "

[8]Again, the devil took him to a very high mountain and showed him all the kingdoms of the world and their splendour. [9]"All this I will give you," he said, "if you will bow down and worship me."

[10]Jesus said to him, "Away from me, Satan! For it is written: 'Worship the Lord your God, and serve him only.'[e] "

[11]Then the devil left him, and angels came and attended him.

Jesus begins to preach

[12]When Jesus heard that John had been put in prison, he withdrew to Galilee. [13]Leaving Nazareth, he went and lived in Capernaum, which was by the lake in the area of Zebulun and Naphtali—[14]to fulfil what was said through the prophet Isaiah:

---

b 4 Deut. 8:3
c 6 Psalm 91:11,12
d 7 Deut. 6:16
e 10 Deut. 6:13

¹⁵"Land of Zebulun and land of Naphtali,
　　the Way of the Sea, beyond the Jordan,
　　Galilee of the Gentiles—
¹⁶the people living in darkness
　　have seen a great light;
　on those living in the land of the shadow of death
　　a light has dawned."[f]

¹⁷From that time on Jesus began to preach, "Repent, for the kingdom of heaven has come near."

Jesus calls his first disciples

¹⁸As Jesus was walking beside the Sea of Galilee, he saw two brothers, Simon called Peter and his brother Andrew. They were casting a net into the lake, for they were fishermen. ¹⁹"Come, follow me," Jesus said, "and I will send you out to fish for people." ²⁰At once they left their nets and followed him.

²¹Going on from there, he saw two other brothers, James son of Zebedee and his brother John. They were in a boat with their father Zebedee, preparing their nets. Jesus called them, ²²and immediately they left the boat and their father and followed him.

Jesus heals the sick

²³Jesus went throughout Galilee, teaching in their synagogues, proclaiming the good news of the kingdom, and healing every disease and illness among the people. ²⁴News about him spread all over Syria, and people brought to him all who were ill with various diseases, those suffering severe

f 16 Isaiah 9:1,2

pain, the demon-possessed, those having seizures, and the paralysed, and he healed them. [25]Large crowds from Galilee, the Decapolis,[g] Jerusalem, Judea and the region across the Jordan followed him.

Introduction to the Sermon on the Mount

5 Now when Jesus saw the crowds, he went up on a mountainside and sat down. His disciples came to him, [2]and he began to teach them.

The Beatitudes

He said:

[3]"Blessed are the poor in spirit,
　　for theirs is the kingdom of heaven.
[4]Blessed are those who mourn,
　　for they will be comforted.
[5]Blessed are the meek,
　　for they will inherit the earth.
[6]Blessed are those who hunger and thirst for righteousness,
　　for they will be filled.
[7]Blessed are the merciful,
　　for they will be shown mercy.
[8]Blessed are the pure in heart,
　　for they will see God.
[9]Blessed are the peacemakers,
　　for they will be called children of God.
[10]Blessed are those who are persecuted because of
　　　righteousness,
　　for theirs is the kingdom of heaven.

---

g 25 That is, the Ten Cities

[11]"Blessed are you when people insult you, persecute you and falsely say all kinds of evil against you because of me. [12]Rejoice and be glad, because great is your reward in heaven, for in the same way they persecuted the prophets who were before you.

Salt and light

[13]"You are the salt of the earth. But if the salt loses its saltiness, how can it be made salty again? It is no longer good for anything, except to be thrown out and trampled underfoot.

[14]"You are the light of the world. A city on a hill cannot be hidden. [15]Neither do people light a lamp and put it under a bowl. Instead they put it on its stand, and it gives light to everyone in the house. [16]In the same way, let your light shine before others, that they may see your good deeds and glorify your Father in heaven.

The fulfilment of the law

[17]"Do not think that I have come to abolish the Law or the Prophets; I have not come to abolish them but to fulfil them. [18]Truly I tell you, until heaven and earth disappear, not the smallest letter, not the least stroke of a pen, will by any means disappear from the Law until everything is accomplished. [19]Anyone who sets aside one of the least of these commandments and teaches others accordingly will be called least in the kingdom of heaven, but whoever practises and teaches these commands will be called great in the kingdom of heaven. [20]For I tell you that unless your righteousness surpasses that of the Pharisees and the teachers of the law, you will certainly not enter the kingdom of heaven.

Murder

[21]"You have heard that it was said to the people long ago, 'You shall not murder,[a] and anyone who murders will be subject to judgment.' [22]But I tell you that anyone who is angry with a brother or sister[b] will be subject to judgment. Again, anyone who says to a brother or sister, 'Raca,'[c] is answerable to the Sanhedrin. And anyone who says, 'You fool!' will be in danger of the fire of hell.

[23]"Therefore, if you are offering your gift at the altar and there remember that a brother or sister has something against you, [24]leave your gift there in front of the altar. First go and be reconciled to that person; then come and offer your gift.

[25]"Settle matters quickly with your adversary who is taking you to court. Do it while you are still together on the way, or your adversary may hand you over to the judge, and the judge may hand you over to the officer, and you may be thrown into prison. [26]Truly I tell you, you will not get out until you have paid the last penny.

Adultery

[27]"You have heard that it was said, 'You shall not commit adultery.'[d] [28]But I tell you that anyone who looks at a woman lustfully has already committed adultery with her in his heart. [29]If your right eye causes you to stumble, gouge it out and throw it away. It is better for you to lose one part of your body than for your whole body to be thrown into hell. [30]And if your right hand causes you to stumble, cut it off and throw it away.

---

a 21 Exodus 20:13
b 22 Some manuscripts *brother or sister without cause*
c 22 An Aramaic term of contempt
d 27 Exodus 20:14

It is better for you to lose one part of your body than for your whole body to go into hell.

Divorce

31"It has been said, 'Anyone who divorces his wife must give her a certificate of divorce.'[e] 32But I tell you that anyone who divorces his wife, except for sexual immorality, causes her to become an adulteress, and anyone who marries the divorced woman commits adultery.

Oaths

33"Again, you have heard that it was said to the people long ago, 'Do not break your oath, but fulfil to the Lord the vows you have made.' 34But I tell you, do not swear an oath at all: either by heaven, for it is God's throne; 35or by the earth, for it is his footstool; or by Jerusalem, for it is the city of the Great King. 36And do not swear by your head, for you cannot make even one hair white or black. 37All you need to say is simply 'Yes,' or 'No'; anything beyond this comes from the evil one.[f]

An eye for an eye

38"You have heard that it was said, 'Eye for eye, and tooth for tooth.'[g] 39But I tell you, do not resist an evil person. If anyone slaps you on the right cheek, turn to them the other cheek also. 40And if anyone wants to sue you and take your shirt, hand over your coat as well. 41If anyone forces you to go one mile, go with them two miles. 42Give to the one who asks you, and do not turn away from the one who wants to borrow from you.

---

e 31 Deut. 24:1
f 37 Or *from evil*
g 38 Exodus 21:24; Lev. 24:20; Deut. 19:21

Love for enemies

[43]"You have heard that it was said, 'Love your neighbour[h] and hate your enemy.' [44]But I tell you, love your enemies and pray for those who persecute you, [45]that you may be children of your Father in heaven. He causes his sun to rise on the evil and the good, and sends rain on the righteous and the unrighteous. [46]If you love those who love you, what reward will you get? Are not even the tax collectors doing that? [47]And if you greet only your own people, what are you doing more than others? Do not even pagans do that? [48]Be perfect, therefore, as your heavenly Father is perfect.

Giving to the needy

6 "Be careful not to do your 'acts of righteousness' in front of others, to be seen by them. If you do, you will have no reward from your Father in heaven.

[2]"So when you give to the needy, do not announce it with trumpets, as the hypocrites do in the synagogues and on the streets, to be honoured by others. Truly I tell you, they have received their reward in full. [3]But when you give to the needy, do not let your left hand know what your right hand is doing, [4]so that your giving may be in secret. Then your Father, who sees what is done in secret, will reward you.

Prayer

[5]"And when you pray, do not be like the hypocrites, for they love to pray standing in the synagogues and on the street corners to be seen by others. Truly I tell you, they have received their reward in full. [6]But when you pray, go into

---

h 43 Lev. 19:18

your room, close the door and pray to your Father, who is unseen. Then your Father, who sees what is done in secret, will reward you. [7]And when you pray, do not keep on babbling like pagans, for they think they will be heard because of their many words. [8]Do not be like them, for your Father knows what you need before you ask him.

[9]"This, then, is how you should pray:

" 'Our Father in heaven,
  hallowed be your name,
[10]your kingdom come,
  your will be done,
    on earth as it is in heaven.
[11]Give us today our daily bread.
[12]And forgive us our debts,
  as we also have forgiven our debtors.
[13]And lead us not into temptation,[a]
  but deliver us from the evil one.[b] '

[14]For if you forgive others when they sin against you, your heavenly Father will also forgive you. [15]But if you do not forgive others their sins, your Father will not forgive your sins.

Fasting

[16]"When you fast, do not look sombre as the hypocrites do, for they disfigure their faces to show others they are fasting. Truly I tell you, they have received their reward in full. [17]But when you fast, put oil on your head and wash your face, [18]so that it will not be obvious to others that you are fasting, but

a 13 The Greek for *temptation* can also mean *testing*.
b 13 Or *from evil*; some late manuscripts *one, / for yours is the kingdom and the power and the glory for ever. Amen.*

only to your Father, who is unseen; and your Father, who sees what is done in secret, will reward you.

Treasures in heaven

[19]"Do not store up for yourselves treasures on earth, where moth and rust destroy, and where thieves break in and steal. [20]But store up for yourselves treasures in heaven, where moth and rust do not destroy, and where thieves do not break in and steal. [21]For where your treasure is, there your heart will be also.

[22]"The eye is the lamp of the body. If your eyes are healthy,[c] your whole body will be full of light. [23]But if your eyes are unhealthy,[d] your whole body will be full of darkness. If then the light within you is darkness, how great is that darkness!

[24]"No-one can serve two masters. Either you will hate the one and love the other, or you will be devoted to the one and despise the other. You cannot serve both God and Money.

Do not worry

[25]"Therefore I tell you, do not worry about your life, what you will eat or drink; or about your body, what you will wear. Is not life more important than food, and the body more important than clothes? [26]Look at the birds of the air; they do not sow or reap or store away in barns, and yet your heavenly Father feeds them. Are you not much more valuable than they? [27]Can any one of you by worrying add a single hour to your life?[e]

[28]"And why do you worry about clothes? See how the flowers of the field grow. They do not labour or spin. [29]Yet I tell you that not even Solomon in all his splendour was

---

c 22 The Greek for *healthy* here implies *generous*.

d 23 The Greek for *unhealthy* here implies *stingy*.

e 27 Or *single cubit to your height*

dressed like one of these. ³⁰If that is how God clothes the grass of the field, which is here today and tomorrow is thrown into the fire, will he not much more clothe you—you of little faith? ³¹So do not worry, saying, 'What shall we eat?' or 'What shall we drink?' or 'What shall we wear?' ³²For the pagans run after all these things, and your heavenly Father knows that you need them. ³³But seek first his kingdom and his righteousness, and all these things will be given to you as well. ³⁴Therefore do not worry about tomorrow, for tomorrow will worry about itself. Each day has enough trouble of its own.

Judging others

7 "Do not judge, or you too will be judged. ²For in the same way as you judge others, you will be judged, and with the measure you use, it will be measured to you.

³"Why do you look at the speck of sawdust in someone else's eye and pay no attention to the plank in your own eye? ⁴How can you say, 'Let me take the speck out of your eye,' when all the time there is a plank in your own eye? ⁵You hypocrite, first take the plank out of your own eye, and then you will see clearly to remove the speck from the other person's eye.

⁶"Do not give dogs what is sacred; do not throw your pearls to pigs. If you do, they may trample them under their feet, and then turn and tear you to pieces.

Ask, seek, knock

⁷"Ask and it will be given to you; seek and you will find; knock and the door will be opened to you. ⁸For everyone who asks receives; those who seek find; and to those who knock, the door will be opened.

⁹"Which of you, if your son asks for bread, will give him a stone? ¹⁰Or if he asks for a fish, will give him a snake? ¹¹If you,

then, though you are evil, know how to give good gifts to your children, how much more will your Father in heaven give good gifts to those who ask him! ¹²So in everything, do to others what you would have them do to you, for this sums up the Law and the Prophets.

The narrow and wide gates

¹³"Enter through the narrow gate. For wide is the gate and broad is the road that leads to destruction, and many enter through it. ¹⁴But small is the gate and narrow the road that leads to life, and only a few find it.

True and false prophets

¹⁵"Watch out for false prophets. They come to you in sheep's clothing, but inwardly they are ferocious wolves. ¹⁶By their fruit you will recognise them. Do people pick grapes from thorn-bushes, or figs from thistles? ¹⁷Likewise, every good tree bears good fruit, but a bad tree bears bad fruit. ¹⁸A good tree cannot bear bad fruit, and a bad tree cannot bear good fruit. ¹⁹Every tree that does not bear good fruit is cut down and thrown into the fire. ²⁰Thus, by their fruit you will recognise them.

True and false disciples

²¹"Not everyone who says to me, 'Lord, Lord,' will enter the kingdom of heaven, but only those who do the will of my Father who is in heaven. ²²Many will say to me on that day, 'Lord, Lord, did we not prophesy in your name and in your name drive out demons and in your name perform many miracles?' ²³Then I will tell them plainly, 'I never knew you. Away from me, you evildoers!'

The wise and foolish builders

24"Therefore everyone who hears these words of mine and puts them into practice is like a wise man who built his house on the rock. 25The rain came down, the streams rose, and the winds blew and beat against that house; yet it did not fall, because it had its foundation on the rock. 26But everyone who hears these words of mine and does not put them into practice is like a foolish man who built his house on sand. 27The rain came down, the streams rose, and the winds blew and beat against that house, and it fell with a great crash."

28When Jesus had finished saying these things, the crowds were amazed at his teaching, 29because he taught as one who had authority, and not as their teachers of the law.

Jesus heals a man with leprosy

8 When Jesus came down from the mountainside, large crowds followed him. 2A man with leprosy[a] came and knelt before him and said, "Lord, if you are willing, you can make me clean."

3Jesus reached out his hand and touched the man. "I am willing," he said. "Be clean!" Immediately he was cleansed of his leprosy. 4Then Jesus said to him, "See that you don't tell anyone. But go, show yourself to the priest and offer the gift Moses commanded, as a testimony to them."

The faith of the centurion

5When Jesus had entered Capernaum, a centurion came to him, asking for help. 6"Lord," he said, "my servant lies at home paralysed, suffering terribly."

---

a 2 The Greek word traditionally translated *leprosy* was used for various diseases affecting the skin.

[7]Jesus said to him, "Shall I come and heal him?"

[8]The centurion replied, "Lord, I do not deserve to have you come under my roof. But just say the word, and my servant will be healed. [9]For I myself am a man under authority, with soldiers under me. I tell this one, 'Go,' and he goes; and that one, 'Come,' and he comes. I say to my servant, 'Do this,' and he does it."

[10]When Jesus heard this, he was amazed and said to those following him, "Truly I tell you, I have not found anyone in Israel with such great faith. [11]I say to you that many will come from the east and the west, and will take their places at the feast with Abraham, Isaac and Jacob in the kingdom of heaven. [12]But the subjects of the kingdom will be thrown outside, into the darkness, where there will be weeping and gnashing of teeth."

[13]Then Jesus said to the centurion, "Go! Let it be done just as you believed it would." And his servant was healed at that very hour.

Jesus heals many

[14]When Jesus came into Peter's house, he saw Peter's mother-in-law lying in bed with a fever. [15]He touched her hand and the fever left her, and she got up and began to wait on him.

[16]When evening came, many who were demon-possessed were brought to him, and he drove out the spirits with a word and healed all who were ill. [17]This was to fulfil what was spoken through the prophet Isaiah:

> "He took up our infirmities
>   and bore our suffering."[b]

---

b 17 Isaiah 53:4

The cost of following Jesus

¹⁸When Jesus saw the crowd around him, he gave orders to cross to the other side of the lake. ¹⁹Then a teacher of the law came to him and said, "Teacher, I will follow you wherever you go."

²⁰Jesus replied, "Foxes have holes and birds have nests, but the Son of Man has nowhere to lay his head."

²¹Another disciple said to him, "Lord, first let me go and bury my father."

²²But Jesus told him, "Follow me, and let the dead bury their own dead."

Jesus calms the storm

²³Then he got into the boat and his disciples followed him. ²⁴Suddenly a furious storm came up on the lake, so that the waves swept over the boat. But Jesus was sleeping. ²⁵The disciples went and woke him, saying, "Lord, save us! We're going to drown!"

²⁶He replied, "You of little faith, why are you so afraid?" Then he got up and rebuked the winds and the waves, and it was completely calm.

²⁷The men were amazed and asked, "What kind of man is this? Even the winds and the waves obey him!"

Jesus restores two demon-possessed men

²⁸When he arrived at the other side in the region of the Gadarenes,ᶜ two demon-possessed men coming from the tombs met him. They were so violent that no-one could pass that way. ²⁹"What do you want with us, Son of God?" they

---

c 28 Some manuscripts *Gergesenes*; other manuscripts *Gerasenes* shouted. "Have you come here to torture us before the appointed time?"

³⁰Some distance from them a large herd of pigs was feeding. ³¹The demons begged Jesus, "If you drive us out, send us into the herd of pigs."

³²He said to them, "Go!" So they came out and went into the pigs, and the whole herd rushed down the steep bank into the lake and died in the water. ³³Those tending the pigs ran off, went into the town and reported all this, including what had happened to the demon-possessed men. ³⁴Then the whole town went out to meet Jesus. And when they saw him, they pleaded with him to leave their region.

Jesus forgives and heals a paralysed man

9 Jesus stepped into a boat, crossed over and came to his own town. ²Some men brought to him a paralysed man, lying on a mat. When Jesus saw their faith, he said to the man, "Take heart, son; your sins are forgiven."

³At this, some of the teachers of the law said to themselves, "This fellow is blaspheming!"

⁴Knowing their thoughts, Jesus said, "Why do you entertain evil thoughts in your hearts? ⁵Which is easier: to say, 'Your sins are forgiven,' or to say, 'Get up and walk'? ⁶But I want you to know that the Son of Man has authority on earth to forgive sins." So he said to the paralysed man, "Get up, take your mat and go home." ⁷Then the man got up and went home. ⁸When the crowd saw this, they were filled with awe; and they praised God, who had given such authority to human beings.

The calling of Matthew

⁹As Jesus went on from there, he saw a man named Matthew sitting at the tax collector's booth. "Follow me,"

he told him, and Matthew got up and followed him.

¹⁰While Jesus was having dinner at Matthew's house, many tax collectors and sinners came and ate with him and his disciples. ¹¹When the Pharisees saw this, they asked his disciples, "Why does your teacher eat with tax collectors and sinners?"

¹²On hearing this, Jesus said, "It is not the healthy who need a doctor, but those who are ill. ¹³But go and learn what this means: 'I desire mercy, not sacrifice.'ᵃ For I have not come to call the righteous, but sinners."

Jesus questioned about fasting

¹⁴Then John's disciples came and asked him, "How is it that we and the Pharisees fast often, but your disciples do not fast?"

¹⁵Jesus answered, "How can the guests of the bridegroom mourn while he is with them? The time will come when the bridegroom will be taken from them; then they will fast.

¹⁶"No-one sews a patch of unshrunk cloth on an old garment, for the patch will pull away from the garment, making the tear worse. ¹⁷Neither do people pour new wine into old wineskins. If they do, the skins will burst; the wine will run out, and the wineskins will be ruined. No, they pour new wine into new wineskins, and both are preserved."

Jesus raises a dead girl and heals a sick woman

¹⁸While he was saying this, a synagogue leader came and knelt before him and said, "My daughter has just died. But come and put your hand on her, and she will live." ¹⁹Jesus got up and went with him, and so did his disciples.

²⁰Just then a woman who had been subject to bleeding for

a 13 Hosea 6:6

twelve years came up behind him and touched the edge of his cloak. [21]She said to herself, "If I only touch his cloak, I will be healed."

[22]Jesus turned and saw her. "Take heart, daughter," he said, "your faith has healed you." And the woman was healed from that moment.

[23]When Jesus entered the synagogue leader's house and saw the pipers and the noisy crowd, [24]he said, "Go away. The girl is not dead but asleep." But they laughed at him. [25]After the crowd had been put outside, he went in and took the girl by the hand, and she got up. [26]News of this spread through all that region.

Jesus heals the blind and mute

[27]As Jesus went on from there, two blind men followed him, calling out, "Have mercy on us, Son of David!"

[28]When he had gone indoors, the blind men came to him, and he asked them, "Do you believe that I am able to do this?"

"Yes, Lord," they replied.

[29]Then he touched their eyes and said, "According to your faith let it be done to you"; [30]and their sight was restored. Jesus warned them sternly, "See that no-one knows about this." [31]But they went out and spread the news about him all over that region.

[32]While they were going out, a man who was demon-possessed and could not talk was brought to Jesus. [33]And when the demon was driven out, the man who had been mute spoke. The crowd was amazed and said, "Nothing like this has ever been seen in Israel."

[34]But the Pharisees said, "It is by the prince of demons that he drives out demons."

The workers are few

[35]Jesus went through all the towns and villages, teaching in their synagogues, proclaiming the good news of the kingdom and healing every disease and illness. [36]When he saw the crowds, he had compassion on them, because they were harassed and helpless, like sheep without a shepherd. [37]Then he said to his disciples, "The harvest is plentiful but the workers are few. [38]Ask the Lord of the harvest, therefore, to send out workers into his harvest field."

Jesus sends out the Twelve

10 Jesus called his twelve disciples to him and gave them authority to drive out evil[a] spirits and to heal every disease and illness.

[2]These are the names of the twelve apostles: first, Simon (who is called Peter) and his brother Andrew; James son of Zebedee, and his brother John; [3]Philip and Bartholomew; Thomas and Matthew the tax collector; James son of Alphaeus, and Thaddaeus; [4]Simon the Zealot and Judas Iscariot, who betrayed him.

[5]These twelve Jesus sent out with the following instructions: "Do not go among the Gentiles or enter any town of the Samaritans. [6]Go rather to the lost sheep of Israel. [7]As you go, proclaim this message: 'The kingdom of heaven has come near.' [8]Heal those who are ill, raise the dead, cleanse those who have leprosy,[b] drive out demons. Freely you have received, freely give.

[9]"Do not get any gold or silver or copper to take with you

a 1 Greek *unclean*
b 8 The Greek word traditionally translated *leprosy* was used for various diseases affecting the skin.

in your belts—[10]no bag for the journey or extra shirt or sandals or a staff, for workers are worth their keep. [11]Whatever town or village you enter, search for some worthy person there and stay at that person's house until you leave. [12]As you enter the home, give it your greeting. [13]If the home is deserving, let your peace rest on it; if it is not, let your peace return to you. [14]If anyone will not welcome you or listen to your words, shake the dust off your feet when you leave that home or town. [15]Truly I tell you, it will be more bearable for Sodom and Gomorrah on the day of judgment than for that town.

[16]"I am sending you out like sheep among wolves. Therefore be as shrewd as snakes and as innocent as doves. [17]Be on your guard; you will be handed over to the local councils and be flogged in the synagogues. [18]On my account you will be brought before governors and kings as witnesses to them and to the Gentiles. [19]But when they arrest you, do not worry about what to say or how to say it. At that time you will be given what to say, [20]for it will not be you speaking, but the Spirit of your Father speaking through you.

[21]"Brother will betray brother to death, and a father his child; children will rebel against their parents and have them put to death. [22]Everyone will hate you because of me, but those who stand firm to the end will be saved. [23]When you are persecuted in one place, flee to another. Truly I tell you, you will not finish going through the towns of Israel before the Son of Man comes.

[24]"Students are not above their teacher, nor servants above their master. [25]It is enough for students to be like their teacher, and servants like their master. If the head of the house has been called Beelzebul, how much more the members of his household!

[26]"So do not be afraid of them. There is nothing concealed that will not be disclosed, or hidden that will not be made known. [27]What I tell you in the dark, speak in the daylight; what is whispered in your ear, proclaim from the roofs. [28]Do not be afraid of those who kill the body but cannot kill the soul. Rather, be afraid of the One who can destroy both soul and body in hell. [29]Are not two sparrows sold for a penny? Yet not one of them will fall to the ground outside your Father's care.[c] [30]And even the very hairs of your head are all numbered. [31]So don't be afraid; you are worth more than many sparrows.

[32]"Whoever publicly acknowledges me I will also acknowledge before my Father in heaven. [33]But whoever publicly disowns me I will disown before my Father in heaven.

[34]"Do not suppose that I have come to bring peace to the earth. I did not come to bring peace, but a sword. [35]For I have come to turn

" 'a man against his father,
    a daughter against her mother,
a daughter-in-law against her mother-in-law—
[36]   your enemies will be the members of your own
        household.'[d]

[37]"Anyone who loves their father or mother more than me is not worthy of me; anyone who loves a son or daughter more than me is not worthy of me. [38]Whoever does not take up their cross and follow me is not worthy of me. [39]Whoever finds their life will lose it, and whoever loses their life for my sake will find it.

---

c 29 Or *will*; or *knowledge*
d 36 Micah 7:6

⁴⁰"Anyone who welcomes you welcomes me, and anyone who welcomes me welcomes the one who sent me. ⁴¹Whoever welcomes someone known to be a prophet will receive a prophet's reward, and whoever welcomes someone known to be righteous will receive a righteous person's reward. ⁴²And if anyone gives even a cup of cold water to one of these little ones who is known to be my disciple, truly I tell you, that person will certainly be rewarded."

Jesus and John the Baptist

11 After Jesus had finished instructing his twelve disciples, he went on from there to teach and preach in the towns of Galilee.ᵃ

²When John heard in prison what the Messiah was doing, he sent his disciples ³to ask him, "Are you the one who was to come, or should we expect someone else?"

⁴Jesus replied, "Go back and report to John what you hear and see: ⁵The blind receive sight, the lame walk, those who have leprosyᵇ are cleansed, the deaf hear, the dead are raised, and the good news is proclaimed to the poor. ⁶Blessed is anyone who does not stumble on account of me."

⁷As John's disciples were leaving, Jesus began to speak to the crowd about John: "What did you go out into the wilderness to see? A reed swayed by the wind? ⁸If not, what did you go out to see? A man dressed in fine clothes? No, those who wear fine clothes are in kings' palaces. ⁹Then what did you go out to see? A prophet? Yes, I tell you, and more than a prophet. ¹⁰This is the one about whom it is written:

---

a 1 Greek *in their towns*
b 5 The Greek word traditionally translated *leprosy* was used for various diseases affecting the skin.

" 'I will send my messenger ahead of you,
   who will prepare your way before you.'[c]

[11]Truly I tell you, among those born of women there has not
risen anyone greater than John the Baptist; yet whoever is
least in the kingdom of heaven is greater than he. [12]From the
days of John the Baptist until now, the kingdom of heaven has
been subjected to violence,[d] and violent people have been
raiding it. [13]For all the Prophets and the Law prophesied until
John. [14]And if you are willing to accept it, he is the Elijah who
was to come. [15]Whoever has ears, let them hear.

[16]"To what can I compare this generation? They are like
children sitting in the market-places and calling out to others:

[17]" 'We played the pipe for you,
      and you did not dance;
   we sang a dirge,
      and you did not mourn.'

[18]For John came neither eating nor drinking, and they say, 'He
has a demon.' [19]The Son of Man came eating and drinking,
and they say, 'Here is a glutton and a drunkard, a friend of tax
collectors and sinners.' But wisdom is proved right by her
actions."

Woe on unrepentant towns

[20]Then Jesus began to denounce the towns in which most
of his miracles had been performed, because they did not
repent. [21]"Woe to you, Chorazin! Woe to you, Bethsaida! If

---

c 10 Mal. 3:1
d 12 Or *been forcefully advancing*

the miracles that were performed in you had been performed in Tyre and Sidon, they would have repented long ago in sackcloth and ashes. [22]But I tell you, it will be more bearable for Tyre and Sidon on the day of judgment than for you. [23]And you, Capernaum, will you be lifted up to the skies? No, you will go down to the depths.[e] If the miracles that were performed in you had been performed in Sodom, it would have remained to this day. [24]But I tell you that it will be more bearable for Sodom on the day of judgment than for you."

The Father revealed in the Son

[25]At that time Jesus said, "I praise you, Father, Lord of heaven and earth, because you have hidden these things from the wise and learned, and revealed them to little children. [26]Yes, Father, for this was your good pleasure.

[27]"All things have been committed to me by my Father. No-one knows the Son except the Father, and no-one knows the Father except the Son and those to whom the Son chooses to reveal him.

[28]"Come to me, all you who are weary and burdened, and I will give you rest. [29]Take my yoke upon you and learn from me, for I am gentle and humble in heart, and you will find rest for your souls. [30]For my yoke is easy and my burden is light."

Jesus is Lord of the Sabbath

12 At that time Jesus went through the cornfields on the Sabbath. His disciples were hungry and began to pick some ears of corn and eat them. [2]When the Pharisees saw this, they said to him, "Look! Your disciples are doing what is unlawful on the Sabbath."

---

e 23 Greek *Hades*

³He answered, "Haven't you read what David did when he and his companions were hungry? ⁴He entered the house of God, and he and his companions ate the consecrated bread—which was not lawful for them to do, but only for the priests. ⁵Or haven't you read in the Law that the priests on Sabbath duty in the temple desecrate the Sabbath and yet are innocent? ⁶I tell you that one[a] greater than the temple is here. ⁷If you had known what these words mean, 'I desire mercy, not sacrifice,'[b] you would not have condemned the innocent. ⁸For the Son of Man is Lord of the Sabbath."

⁹Going on from that place, he went into their synagogue, ¹⁰and a man with a shrivelled hand was there. Looking for a reason to accuse Jesus, they asked him, "Is it lawful to heal on the Sabbath?"

¹¹He said to them, "If any of you has a sheep and it falls into a pit on the Sabbath, will you not take hold of it and lift it out? ¹²How much more valuable is a human being than a sheep! Therefore it is lawful to do good on the Sabbath."

¹³Then he said to the man, "Stretch out your hand." So he stretched it out and it was completely restored, just as sound as the other. ¹⁴But the Pharisees went out and plotted how they might kill Jesus.

God's chosen servant

¹⁵Aware of this, Jesus withdrew from that place. A large crowd followed him, and he healed all who were ill. ¹⁶He warned them not to tell others about him. ¹⁷This was to fulfil what was spoken through the prophet Isaiah:

a 6 Or *something*; also in verses 41 and 42
b 7 Hosea 6:6

¹⁸"Here is my servant whom I have chosen,
   the one I love, in whom I delight;
I will put my Spirit on him,
   and he will proclaim justice to the nations.
¹⁹He will not quarrel or cry out;
   no-one will hear his voice in the streets.
²⁰A bruised reed he will not break,
   and a smouldering wick he will not snuff out,
   till he leads justice to victory.
²¹   In his name the nations will put their hope."^c

Jesus and Beelzebul

²²Then they brought him a demon-possessed man who was blind and mute, and Jesus healed him, so that he could both talk and see. ²³All the people were astonished and said, "Could this be the Son of David?"

²⁴But when the Pharisees heard this, they said, "It is only by Beelzebul, the prince of demons, that this fellow drives out demons."

²⁵Jesus knew their thoughts and said to them, "Every kingdom divided against itself will be ruined, and every city or household divided against itself will not stand. ²⁶If Satan drives out Satan, he is divided against himself. How then can his kingdom stand? ²⁷And if I drive out demons by Beelzebul, by whom do your people drive them out? So then, they will be your judges. ²⁸But if it is by the Spirit of God that I drive out demons, then the kingdom of God has come to you.

²⁹"Or again, how can anyone enter a strong man's house and carry off his possessions without first tying up the strong man? Then his house can be plundered.

---

c 21 Isaiah 42:1–4

³⁰"Whoever is not with me is against me, and whoever does not gather with me scatters. ³¹And so I tell you, people will be forgiven every sin and blasphemy. But blasphemy against the Spirit will not be forgiven. ³²Anyone who speaks a word against the Son of Man will be forgiven, but anyone who speaks against the Holy Spirit will not be forgiven, either in this age or in the age to come.

³³"Make a tree good and its fruit will be good, or make a tree bad and its fruit will be bad, for a tree is recognised by its fruit. ³⁴You brood of vipers, how can you who are evil say anything good? For out of the overflow of the heart the mouth speaks. ³⁵Good people bring good things out of the good stored up in them, and evil people bring evil things out of the evil stored up in them. ³⁶But I tell you that people will have to give account on the day of judgment for every empty word they have spoken. ³⁷For by your words you will be acquitted, and by your words you will be condemned."

The sign of Jonah

³⁸Then some of the Pharisees and teachers of the law said to him, "Teacher, we want to see a sign from you."

³⁹He answered, "A wicked and adulterous generation asks for a sign! But none will be given it except the sign of the prophet Jonah. ⁴⁰For as Jonah was three days and three nights in the belly of a huge fish, so the Son of Man will be three days and three nights in the heart of the earth. ⁴¹The people of Nineveh will stand up at the judgment with this generation and condemn it; for they repented at the preaching of Jonah, and now one^d greater than Jonah is here. ⁴²The Queen of the South will rise at the judgment with this generation and

---

d 41 Or *something*; also in verse 42

condemn it; for she came from the ends of the earth to listen to Solomon's wisdom, and now one greater than Solomon is here.

⁴³"When an evil^e spirit comes out of anyone, it goes through arid places seeking rest and does not find it. ⁴⁴Then it says, 'I will return to the house I left.' When it arrives, it finds the house unoccupied, swept clean and put in order. ⁴⁵Then it goes and takes with it seven other spirits more wicked than itself, and they go in and live there. And the final condition of that person is worse than the first. That is how it will be with this wicked generation."

Jesus' mother and brothers

⁴⁶While Jesus was still talking to the crowd, his mother and brothers stood outside, wanting to speak to him. ⁴⁷Someone told him, "Your mother and brothers are standing outside, wanting to speak to you."⁴⁸He replied to him, "Who is my mother, and who are my brothers?" ⁴⁹Pointing to his disciples, he said, "Here are my mother and my brothers. ⁵⁰For whoever does the will of my Father in heaven is my brother and sister and mother."

The parable of the sower

13 That same day Jesus went out of the house and sat by the lake. ²Such large crowds gathered round him that he got into a boat and sat in it, while all the people stood on the shore. ³Then he told them many things in parables, saying: "A farmer went out to sow his seed. ⁴As he was scattering the seed, some fell along the path, and the birds came and ate it up. ⁵Some fell on rocky places, where it did not

---

e 43 Greek *unclean*

have much soil. It sprang up quickly, because the soil was shallow. [6]But when the sun came up, the plants were scorched, and they withered because they had no root. [7]Other seed fell among thorns, which grew up and choked the plants. [8]Still other seed fell on good soil, where it produced a crop—a hundred, sixty or thirty times what was sown. [9]Whoever has ears, let them hear."

[10]The disciples came to him and asked, "Why do you speak to the people in parables?"

[11]He replied, "The knowledge of the secrets of the kingdom of heaven has been given to you, but not to them. [12]Those who have will be given more, and they will have an abundance. As for those who do not have, even what they have will be taken from them. [13]This is why I speak to them in parables:

"Though seeing, they do not see;
　though hearing, they do not hear or understand.

[14]In them is fulfilled the prophecy of Isaiah:

" 'You will be ever hearing but never understanding;
　you will be ever seeing but never perceiving.
[15]For this people's heart has become calloused;
　they hardly hear with their ears,
　and they have closed their eyes.
Otherwise they might see with their eyes,
　hear with their ears,
　understand with their hearts
and turn, and I would heal them.'[a]

---

a 15 Isaiah 6:9,10 (see Septuagint)

[16]But blessed are your eyes because they see, and your ears because they hear. [17]Truly I tell you, many prophets and righteous people longed to see what you see but did not see it, and to hear what you hear but did not hear it.

[18]"Listen then to what the parable of the sower means: [19]When people hear the message about the kingdom and do not understand it, the evil one comes and snatches away what was sown in their hearts. This is the seed sown along the path. [20]The seed falling on rocky ground refers to people who hear the word and at once receive it with joy. [21]But since they have no root, they last only a short time. When trouble or persecution comes because of the word, they quickly fall away. [22]The seed falling among the thorns refers to people who hear the word, but the worries of this life and the deceitfulness of wealth choke the word, making it unfruitful. [23]But seed falling on good soil refers to people who hear the word and understand it. They produce a crop, yielding a hundred, sixty or thirty times what was sown."

The parable of the weeds

[24]Jesus told them another parable: "The kingdom of heaven is like a man who sowed good seed in his field. [25]But while everyone was sleeping, his enemy came and sowed weeds among the wheat, and went away. [26]When the wheat sprouted and formed ears, then the weeds also appeared.

[27]"The owner's servants came to him and said, 'Sir, didn't you sow good seed in your field? Where then did the weeds come from?'

[28]"'An enemy did this,' he replied.

"The servants asked him, 'Do you want us to go and pull them up?'

[29]"'No,' he answered, 'because while you are pulling the

weeds, you may uproot the wheat with them. [30]Let both grow together until the harvest. At that time I will tell the harvesters: First collect the weeds and tie them in bundles to be burned; then gather the wheat and bring it into my barn.' "

The parables of the mustard seed and the yeast

[31]He told them another parable: "The kingdom of heaven is like a mustard seed, which a man took and planted in his field. [32]Though it is the smallest of all seeds, yet when it grows, it is the largest of garden plants and becomes a tree, so that the birds come and perch in its branches."

[33]He told them still another parable: "The kingdom of heaven is like yeast that a woman took and mixed into about eight kilograms of flour until it worked all through the dough."

[34]Jesus spoke all these things to the crowd in parables; he did not say anything to them without using a parable. [35]So was fulfilled what was spoken through the prophet:

"I will open my mouth in parables,
   I will utter things hidden since the creation of the
      world."[b]

The parable of the weeds explained

[36]Then he left the crowd and went into the house. His disciples came to him and said, "Explain to us the parable of the weeds in the field."

[37]He answered, "The one who sowed the good seed is the Son of Man. [38]The field is the world, and the good seed stands for the people of the kingdom. The weeds are the people of the

---

b 35 Psalm 78:2

evil one, [39]and the enemy who sows them is the devil. The harvest is the end of the age, and the harvesters are angels.

[40]"As the weeds are pulled up and burned in the fire, so it will be at the end of the age. [41]The Son of Man will send out his angels, and they will weed out of his kingdom everything that causes sin and all who do evil. [42]They will throw them into the blazing furnace, where there will be weeping and gnashing of teeth. [43]Then the righteous will shine like the sun in the kingdom of their Father. Whoever has ears, let them hear.

The parables of the hidden treasure and the pearl

[44]"The kingdom of heaven is like treasure hidden in a field. When a man found it, he hid it again, and then in his joy went and sold all he had and bought that field.

[45]"Again, the kingdom of heaven is like a merchant looking for fine pearls. [46]When he found one of great value, he went away and sold everything he had and bought it.

The parable of the net

[47]"Once again, the kingdom of heaven is like a net that was let down into the lake and caught all kinds of fish. [48]When it was full, the fishermen pulled it up on the shore. Then they sat down and collected the good fish in baskets, but threw the bad away. [49]This is how it will be at the end of the age. The angels will come and separate the wicked from the righteous [50]and throw them into the blazing furnace, where there will be weeping and gnashing of teeth.

[51]"Have you understood all these things?" Jesus asked.

"Yes," they replied.

[52]He said to them, "Therefore every teacher of the law who has been instructed about the kingdom of heaven is like the

owner of a house who brings out of his storeroom new treasures as well as old."

A prophet without honour

⁵³When Jesus had finished these parables, he moved on from there. ⁵⁴Coming to his home town, he began teaching the people in their synagogue, and they were amazed. "Where did this man get this wisdom and these miraculous powers?" they asked. ⁵⁵"Isn't this the carpenter's son? Isn't his mother's name Mary, and aren't his brothers James, Joseph, Simon and Judas? ⁵⁶Aren't all his sisters with us? Where then did this man get all these things?" ⁵⁷And they took offence at him.

But Jesus said to them, "Only in their own towns and in their own homes are prophets without honour."

⁵⁸And he did not do many miracles there because of their lack of faith.

John the Baptist beheaded

14 At that time Herod the tetrarch heard the reports about Jesus, ²and he said to his attendants, "This is John the Baptist; he has risen from the dead! That is why miraculous powers are at work in him."

³Now Herod had arrested John and bound him and put him in prison because of Herodias, his brother Philip's wife, ⁴for John had been saying to him: "It is not lawful for you to have her." ⁵Herod wanted to kill John, but he was afraid of the people, because they considered him a prophet.

⁶On Herod's birthday the daughter of Herodias danced for them and pleased Herod so much ⁷that he promised with an oath to give her whatever she asked. ⁸Prompted by her mother, she said, "Give me here on a platter the head of John the Baptist." ⁹The king was distressed, but because of his oaths

and his dinner guests, he ordered that her request be granted ¹⁰and had John beheaded in the prison. ¹¹His head was brought in on a platter and given to the girl, who carried it to her mother. ¹²John's disciples came and took his body and buried it. Then they went and told Jesus.

Jesus feeds the five thousand

¹³When Jesus heard what had happened, he withdrew by boat privately to a solitary place. Hearing of this, the crowds followed him on foot from the towns. ¹⁴When Jesus landed and saw a large crowd, he had compassion on them and healed those who were ill.

¹⁵As evening approached, the disciples came to him and said, "This is a remote place, and it's already getting late. Send the crowds away, so that they can go to the villages and buy themselves some food."

¹⁶Jesus replied, "They do not need to go away. You give them something to eat."

¹⁷"We have here only five loaves of bread and two fish," they answered.

¹⁸"Bring them here to me," he said. ¹⁹And he told the people to sit down on the grass. Taking the five loaves and the two fish and looking up to heaven, he gave thanks and broke the loaves. Then he gave them to the disciples, and the disciples gave them to the people. ²⁰They all ate and were satisfied, and the disciples picked up twelve basketfuls of broken pieces that were left over. ²¹The number of those who ate was about five thousand men, besides women and children.

Jesus walks on the water

²²Immediately Jesus made the disciples get into the boat and go on ahead of him to the other side, while he dismissed the crowd.

²³After he had dismissed them, he went up on a mountainside by himself to pray. When evening came, he was there alone, ²⁴but the boat was already a considerable distance from land, buffeted by the waves because the wind was against it.

²⁵Shortly before dawn Jesus went out to them, walking on the lake. ²⁶When the disciples saw him walking on the lake, they were terrified. "It's a ghost," they said, and cried out in fear.

²⁷But Jesus immediately said to them: "Take courage! It is I. Don't be afraid."

²⁸"Lord, if it's you," Peter replied, "tell me to come to you on the water."

²⁹"Come," he said.

Then Peter got down out of the boat, walked on the water and came towards Jesus. ³⁰But when he saw the wind, he was afraid and, beginning to sink, cried out, "Lord, save me!"

³¹Immediately Jesus reached out his hand and caught him. "You of little faith," he said, "why did you doubt?"

³²And when they climbed into the boat, the wind died down. ³³Then those who were in the boat worshipped him, saying, "Truly you are the Son of God."

³⁴When they had crossed over, they landed at Gennesaret. ³⁵And when the men of that place recognised Jesus, they sent word to all the surrounding country. People brought all who were ill to him ³⁶and begged him to let those who were ill just touch the edge of his cloak, and all who touched him were healed.

That which defiles

15 Then some Pharisees and teachers of the law came to Jesus from Jerusalem and asked, ²"Why do your disciples break the tradition of the elders? They don't wash their hands before they eat!"

³Jesus replied, "And why do you break the command of God for the sake of your tradition? ⁴For God said, 'Honour your father and mother'ᵃ and 'Anyone who curses their father or mother is to be put to death.'ᵇ ⁵But you say that if anyone declares that what might have been used to help their father or mother is 'devoted to God,' ⁶they are not to 'honour their father or mother' with it. Thus you nullify the word of God for the sake of your tradition. ⁷You hypocrites! Isaiah was right when he prophesied about you:

⁸" 'These people honour me with their lips,
    but their hearts are far from me.
⁹They worship me in vain;
    their teachings are merely human rules.'ᶜ"

¹⁰Jesus called the crowd to him and said, "Listen and understand. ¹¹What goes into your mouth does not defile you, but what comes out of your mouth, that is what defiles you."

¹²Then the disciples came to him and asked, "Do you know that the Pharisees were offended when they heard this?"

¹³He replied, "Every plant that my heavenly Father has not planted will be pulled up by the roots. ¹⁴Leave them; they are blind guides.ᵈ If the blind lead the blind, both will fall into a pit."

¹⁵Peter said, "Explain the parable to us."

¹⁶"Are you still so dull?" Jesus asked them. ¹⁷"Don't you see that whatever enters the mouth goes into the stomach and then out of the body? ¹⁸But the things that come out of the

---

a 4 Exodus 20:12; Deut. 5:16
b 4 Exodus 21:17; Lev. 20:9
c 9 Isaiah 29:13
d 14 Some manuscripts *blind guides of the blind*

mouth come from the heart, and these defile you. [19]For out of the heart come evil thoughts, murder, adultery, sexual immorality, theft, false testimony, slander. [20]These are what defile you; but eating with unwashed hands does not defile you."

The faith of the Canaanite woman

[21]Leaving that place, Jesus withdrew to the region of Tyre and Sidon. [22]A Canaanite woman from that vicinity came to him, crying out, "Lord, Son of David, have mercy on me! My daughter is demon-possessed and suffering terribly."

[23]Jesus did not answer a word. So his disciples came to him and urged him, "Send her away, for she keeps crying out after us."

[24]He answered, "I was sent only to the lost sheep of Israel."

[25]The woman came and knelt before him. "Lord, help me!" she said.

[26]He replied, "It is not right to take the children's bread and toss it to the dogs."

[27]"Yes it is, Lord," she said. "Even the dogs eat the crumbs that fall from their master's table."

[28]Then Jesus said to her, "Woman,[e] you have great faith! Your request is granted." And her daughter was healed from that very hour.

Jesus feeds the four thousand

[29]Jesus left there and went along the Sea of Galilee. Then he went up on a mountainside and sat down. [30]Great crowds came to him, bringing the lame, the blind, the crippled, the mute and many others, and laid them at his feet; and he healed them. [31]The people were amazed when they saw the

---

e 28 The Greek for *Woman* does not denote any disrespect.

mute speaking, the crippled made well, the lame walking and the blind seeing. And they praised the God of Israel.

[32]Jesus called his disciples to him and said, "I have compassion for these people; they have already been with me three days and have nothing to eat. I do not want to send them away hungry, or they may collapse on the way."

[33]His disciples answered, "Where could we get enough bread in this remote place to feed such a crowd?"

[34]"How many loaves do you have?" Jesus asked.

"Seven," they replied, "and a few small fish."

[35]He told the crowd to sit down on the ground. [36]Then he took the seven loaves and the fish, and when he had given thanks, he broke them and gave them to the disciples, and they in turn to the people. [37]They all ate and were satisfied. Afterwards the disciples picked up seven basketfuls of broken pieces that were left over. [38]The number of those who ate was four thousand men, besides women and children. [39]After Jesus had sent the crowd away, he got into the boat and went to the vicinity of Magadan.

The demand for a sign

16 The Pharisees and Sadducees came to Jesus and tested him by asking him to show them a sign from heaven.

[2]He replied,[a] "When evening comes, you say, 'It will be fair weather, for the sky is red,' [3]and in the morning, 'Today it will be stormy, for the sky is red and overcast.' You know how to interpret the appearance of the sky, but you cannot interpret the signs of the times. [4]A wicked and adulterous generation looks for a sign, but none will be given it except the sign of Jonah." Jesus then left them and went away.

---

a 2 Some early manuscripts do not have the rest of verse 2 and all of verse 3.

The yeast of the Pharisees and Sadducees

[5]When they went across the lake, the disciples forgot to take bread. [6]"Be careful," Jesus said to them. "Be on your guard against the yeast of the Pharisees and Sadducees."

[7]They discussed this among themselves and said, "It is because we didn't bring any bread."

[8]Aware of their discussion, Jesus asked, "You of little faith, why are you talking among yourselves about having no bread? [9]Do you still not understand? Don't you remember the five loaves for the five thousand, and how many basketfuls you gathered? [10]Or the seven loaves for the four thousand, and how many basketfuls you gathered? [11]How is it you don't understand that I was not talking to you about bread? But be on your guard against the yeast of the Pharisees and Sadducees." [12]Then they understood that he was not telling them to guard against the yeast used in bread, but against the teaching of the Pharisees and Sadducees.

Peter declares that Jesus is the Messiah

[13]When Jesus came to the region of Caesarea Philippi, he asked his disciples, "Who do people say the Son of Man is?"

[14]They replied, "Some say John the Baptist; others say Elijah; and still others, Jeremiah or one of the prophets."

[15]"But what about you?" he asked. "Who do you say I am?"

[16]Simon Peter answered, "You are the Messiah, the Son of the living God."

[17]Jesus replied, "Blessed are you, Simon son of Jonah, for this was not revealed to you by flesh and blood, but by my Father in heaven. [18]And I tell you that you are Peter,[b] and on

---

b 18 *Peter* means *rock.*

this rock I will build my church, and the gates of death[c] will not overcome it. [19]I will give you the keys of the kingdom of heaven; whatever you bind on earth will be[d] bound in heaven, and whatever you loose on earth will be[e] loosed in heaven." [20]Then he ordered his disciples not to tell anyone that he was the Messiah.

Jesus predicts his death

[21]From that time on Jesus began to explain to his disciples that he must go to Jerusalem and suffer many things at the hands of the elders, the chief priests and the teachers of the law, and that he must be killed and on the third day be raised to life.

[22]Peter took him aside and began to rebuke him. "Never, Lord!" he said. "This shall never happen to you!"

[23]Jesus turned and said to Peter, "Get behind me, Satan! You are a stumbling-block to me; you do not have in mind the concerns of God, but merely human concerns."

[24]Then Jesus said to his disciples, "Whoever wants to be my disciple must deny themselves and take up their cross and follow me. [25]For whoever wants to save their life[f] will lose it, but whoever loses their life for me will find it. [26]What good will it be for you to gain the whole world, yet forfeit your soul? Or what can you give in exchange for your soul? [27]For the Son of Man is going to come in his Father's glory with his angels, and then he will reward everyone according to what they have done. [28]Truly I tell you, some who are standing here will not taste death before they see the Son of Man coming in his kingdom."

---

c 18 Greek *Hades*
d 19 Or *have been*
e 19 Or *have been*
f 25 The Greek word means either *life* or *soul*; also in verse 26.

The transfiguration

17 After six days Jesus took with him Peter, James and John the brother of James, and led them up a high mountain by themselves. ²There he was transfigured before them. His face shone like the sun, and his clothes became as white as the light. ³Just then there appeared before them Moses and Elijah, talking with Jesus.

⁴Peter said to Jesus, "Lord, it is good for us to be here. If you wish, I will put up three shelters—one for you, one for Moses and one for Elijah."

⁵While he was still speaking, a bright cloud covered them, and a voice from the cloud said, "This is my Son, whom I love; with him I am well pleased. Listen to him!"

⁶When the disciples heard this, they fell face down to the ground, terrified. ⁷But Jesus came and touched them. "Get up," he said. "Don't be afraid." ⁸When they looked up, they saw no-one except Jesus.

⁹As they were coming down the mountain, Jesus instructed them, "Don't tell anyone what you have seen, until the Son of Man has been raised from the dead."

¹⁰The disciples asked him, "Why then do the teachers of the law say that Elijah must come first?"

¹¹Jesus replied, "To be sure, Elijah comes and will restore all things. ¹²But I tell you, Elijah has already come, and they did not recognise him, but have done to him everything they wished. In the same way the Son of Man is going to suffer at their hands." ¹³Then the disciples understood that he was talking to them about John the Baptist.

Jesus heals a demon-possessed boy

¹⁴When they came to the crowd, a man approached Jesus and knelt before him. ¹⁵"Lord, have mercy on my son," he

said. "He has seizures and is suffering greatly. He often falls into the fire or into the water. [16]I brought him to your disciples, but they could not heal him."

[17]"You unbelieving and perverse generation," Jesus replied, "how long shall I stay with you? How long shall I put up with you? Bring the boy here to me." [18]Jesus rebuked the demon, and it came out of the boy, and he was healed from that moment.

[19]Then the disciples came to Jesus in private and asked, "Why couldn't we drive it out?"

[20] [21]He replied, "Because you have so little faith. Truly I tell you, if you have faith as small as a mustard seed, you can say to this mountain, 'Move from here to there' and it will move. Nothing will be impossible for you."

Jesus predicts his death a second time

[22]When they came together in Galilee, he said to them, "The Son of Man is going to be delivered over to human hands. [23]He will be killed, and on the third day he will be raised to life." And the disciples were filled with grief.

The temple tax

[24]After Jesus and his disciples arrived in Capernaum, the collectors of the two-drachma temple tax came to Peter and asked, "Doesn't your teacher pay the temple tax?"

[25]"Yes, he does," he replied.

When Peter came into the house, Jesus was the first to speak. "What do you think, Simon?" he asked. "From whom do the kings of the earth collect duty and taxes—from their own children or from others?"

[26]"From others," Peter answered.

"Then the children are exempt," Jesus said to him. [27]"But so that we may not cause offence, go to the lake and throw out your line. Take the first fish you catch; open its mouth and you will find a four-drachma coin. Take it and give it to them for my tax and yours."

The greatest in the kingdom of heaven

18 At that time the disciples came to Jesus and asked, "Who, then, is the greatest in the kingdom of heaven?" ²He called a little child whom he placed among them. ³And he said: "Truly I tell you, unless you change and become like little children, you will never enter the kingdom of heaven. ⁴Therefore, whoever takes a humble place—becoming like this child—is the greatest in the kingdom of heaven. ⁵And whoever welcomes one such child in my name welcomes me.

Causing to stumble

⁶"If anyone causes one of these little ones—those who believe in me—to stumble, it would be better for them if a large millstone were hung round their neck and they were drowned in the depths of the sea. ⁷Woe to the world because of the things that cause people to stumble! Such things must come, but woe to the person through whom they come! ⁸If your hand or your foot causes you to stumble, cut it off and throw it away. It is better for you to enter life maimed or crippled than to have two hands or two feet and be thrown into eternal fire. ⁹And if your eye causes you to stumble, gouge it out and throw it away. It is better for you to enter life with one eye than to have two eyes and be thrown into the fire of hell.

The parable of the wandering sheep

¹⁰ [¹¹]"See that you do not despise one of these little ones. For I tell you that their angels in heaven always see the face of my Father in heaven.

12"What do you think? If a man owns a hundred sheep, and one of them wanders away, will he not leave the ninety-nine on the hills and go to look for the one that wandered off? 13And if he finds it, truly I tell you, he is happier about that one sheep than about the ninety-nine that did not wander off. 14In the same way your Father in heaven is not willing that any of these little ones should perish.

Dealing with sin in the church

15"If a brother or sister sins,[a] go and point out the fault, just between the two of you. If they listen to you, you have won them over. 16But if they will not listen, take one or two others along, so that 'every matter may be established by the testimony of two or three witnesses.'[b] 17If they still refuse to listen, tell it to the church; and if they refuse to listen even to the church, treat them as you would a pagan or a tax collector.

18"Truly I tell you, whatever you bind on earth will be[c] bound in heaven, and whatever you loose on earth will be[d] loosed in heaven.

19"Again, truly I tell you that if two of you on earth agree about anything you ask for, it will be done for you by my Father in heaven. 20For where two or three come together in my name, there am I with them."

The parable of the unmerciful servant

21Then Peter came to Jesus and asked, "Lord, how many times shall I forgive someone who sins against me? Up to seven times?"

a 15 Some manuscripts *sins against you*
b 16 Deut. 19:15
c 18 Or *have been*
d 18 Or *have been*

²²Jesus answered, "I tell you, not seven times, but seventy-seven times.ᵉ

²³"Therefore, the kingdom of heaven is like a king who wanted to settle accounts with his servants. ²⁴As he began the settlement, a man who owed him ten thousand bags of goldᶠ was brought to him. ²⁵Since he was not able to pay, the master ordered that he and his wife and his children and all that he had be sold to repay the debt.

²⁶"The servant fell on his knees before him. 'Be patient with me,' he begged, 'and I will pay back everything.' ²⁷The servant's master took pity on him, cancelled the debt and let him go.

²⁸"But when that servant went out, he found one of his fellow-servants who owed him a hundred silver coins.ᵍ He grabbed him and began to choke him. 'Pay back what you owe me!' he demanded.

²⁹"His fellow-servant fell to his knees and begged him, 'Be patient with me, and I will pay you back.'

³⁰"But he refused. Instead, he went off and had the man thrown into prison until he could pay the debt. ³¹When the other servants saw what had happened, they were greatly distressed and went and told their master everything that had happened.

³²"Then the master called the servant in. 'You wicked servant,' he said, 'I cancelled all that debt of yours because you begged me to. ³³Shouldn't you have had mercy on your fellow-servant just as I had on you?' ³⁴In anger his master

---

e 22 Or *seventy times seven*

f 24 Greek *ten thousand talents*; a talent was worth about 20 years of a day labourer's wages.

g 28 Greek *a hundred denarii*; a denarius was the daily wage of a day labourer (see Matt. 20:2).

handed him over to the jailers to be tortured, until he should pay back all he owed.

[35]"This is how my heavenly Father will treat each of you unless you forgive a brother or sister from your heart."

Divorce

19 When Jesus had finished saying these things, he left Galilee and went into the region of Judea to the other side of the Jordan. [2]Large crowds followed him, and he healed them there.

[3]Some Pharisees came to him to test him. They asked, "Is it lawful for a man to divorce his wife for any and every reason?"

[4]"Haven't you read," he replied, "that at the beginning the Creator 'made them male and female,'[a] [5]and said, 'For this reason a man will leave his father and mother and be united to his wife, and the two will become one flesh'[b]? [6]So they are no longer two, but one. Therefore what God has joined together, let no-one separate."

[7]"Why then," they asked, "did Moses command that a man give his wife a certificate of divorce and send her away?"

[8]Jesus replied, "Moses permitted you to divorce your wives because your hearts were hard. But it was not this way from the beginning. [9]I tell you that anyone who divorces his wife, except for sexual immorality, and marries another woman commits adultery."

[10]The disciples said to him, "If this is the situation between a husband and wife, it is better not to marry."

[11]Jesus replied, "Not everyone can accept this word, but only those to whom it has been given. [12]For some are eunuchs because they were born that way; others have been made

a 4 Gen. 1:27
b 5 Gen. 2:24

eunuchs; and others have renounced marriage[c] because of the kingdom of heaven. The one who can accept this should accept it."

The little children and Jesus

¹³Then people brought little children to Jesus for him to place his hands on them and pray for them. But the disciples rebuked them.

¹⁴Jesus said, "Let the little children come to me, and do not hinder them, for the kingdom of heaven belongs to such as these." ¹⁵When he had placed his hands on them, he went on from there.

The rich and the kingdom of God

¹⁶Just then a man came up to Jesus and asked, "Teacher, what good thing must I do to get eternal life?"

¹⁷"Why do you ask me about what is good?" Jesus replied. "There is only One who is good. If you want to enter life, keep the commandments."

¹⁸"Which ones?" he enquired.

Jesus replied, " 'You shall not murder, you shall not commit adultery, you shall not steal, you shall not give false testimony, ¹⁹honour your father and mother,'[d] and 'love your neighbour as yourself.'[e] "

²⁰"All these I have kept," the young man said. "What do I still lack?"

²¹Jesus answered, "If you want to be perfect, go, sell your possessions and give to the poor, and you will have treasure in heaven. Then come, follow me."

c 12 Or *have made themselves eunuchs*
d 19 Exodus 20:12–16; Deut. 5:16–20
e 19 Lev. 19:18

²²When the young man heard this, he went away sad, because he had great wealth.

²³Then Jesus said to his disciples, "Truly I tell you, it is hard for the rich to enter the kingdom of heaven. ²⁴Again I tell you, it is easier for a camel to go through the eye of a needle than for the rich to enter the kingdom of God."

²⁵When the disciples heard this, they were greatly astonished and asked, "Who then can be saved?"

²⁶Jesus looked at them and said, "With human beings this is impossible, but with God all things are possible."

²⁷Peter answered him, "We have left everything to follow you! What then will there be for us?"

²⁸Jesus said to them, "Truly I tell you, at the renewal of all things, when the Son of Man sits on his glorious throne, you who have followed me will also sit on twelve thrones, judging the twelve tribes of Israel. ²⁹And everyone who has left houses or brothers or sisters or father or mother or wife[f] or children or fields for my sake will receive a hundred times as much and will inherit eternal life. ³⁰But many who are first will be last, and many who are last will be first.

The parable of the workers in the vineyard

20 "For the kingdom of heaven is like a landowner who went out early in the morning to hire workers for his vineyard. ²He agreed to pay them a denarius for the day and sent them into his vineyard.

³"About nine in the morning he went out and saw others standing in the market-place doing nothing. ⁴He told them, 'You also go and work in my vineyard, and I will pay you whatever is right.' ⁵So they went.

---

f 29 Some manuscripts do not have *or wife*

"He went out again about noon and about three in the afternoon and did the same thing. [6]About five in the afternoon he went out and found still others standing around. He asked them, 'Why have you been standing here all day long doing nothing?'

[7] 'Because no-one has hired us,' they answered.

"He said to them, 'You also go and work in my vineyard.'

[8]"When evening came, the owner of the vineyard said to his supervisor, 'Call the workers and pay them their wages, beginning with the last ones hired and going on to the first.'

[9]"The workers who were hired about five in the afternoon came and each received a denarius. [10]So when those came who were hired first, they expected to receive more. But each one of them also received a denarius. [11]When they received it, they began to grumble against the landowner. [12]'These men who were hired last worked only one hour,' they said, 'and you have made them equal to us who have borne the burden of the work and the heat of the day.'

[13]"But he answered one of them, 'Friend, I am not being unfair to you. Didn't you agree to work for a denarius? [14]Take your pay and go. I want to give the one who was hired last the same as I gave you. [15]Don't I have the right to do what I want with my own money? Or are you envious because I am generous?'

[16]"So the last will be first, and the first will be last."

Jesus predicts his death a third time

[17]Now Jesus was going up to Jerusalem. On the way, he took the Twelve aside and said to them, [18]"We are going up to Jerusalem, and the Son of Man will be delivered over to the chief priests and the teachers of the law. They will condemn him to death [19]and will hand him over to the Gentiles to be

mocked and flogged and crucified. On the third day he will be raised to life!"

A mother's request

²⁰Then the mother of Zebedee's sons came to Jesus with her sons and, kneeling down, asked a favour of him.

²¹"What is it you want?" he asked.

She said, "Grant that one of these two sons of mine may sit at your right and the other at your left in your kingdom."

²²"You don't know what you are asking," Jesus said to them. "Can you drink the cup I am going to drink?"

"We can," they answered.

²³Jesus said to them, "You will indeed drink from my cup, but to sit at my right or left is not for me to grant. These places belong to those for whom they have been prepared by my Father."

²⁴When the ten heard about this, they were indignant with the two brothers. ²⁵Jesus called them together and said, "You know that the rulers of the Gentiles lord it over them, and their high officials exercise authority over them. ²⁶Not so with you. Instead, whoever wants to become great among you must be your servant, ²⁷and whoever wants to be first must be your slave— ²⁸just as the Son of Man did not come to be served, but to serve, and to give his life as a ransom for many."

Two blind men receive sight

²⁹As Jesus and his disciples were leaving Jericho, a large crowd followed him. ³⁰Two blind men were sitting by the roadside, and when they heard that Jesus was going by, they shouted, "Lord, Son of David, have mercy on us!"

³¹The crowd rebuked them and told them to be quiet, but

they shouted all the louder, "Lord, Son of David, have mercy on us!"

³²Jesus stopped and called them. "What do you want me to do for you?" he asked.

³³"Lord," they answered, "we want our sight."

³⁴Jesus had compassion on them and touched their eyes. Immediately they received their sight and followed him.

Jesus comes to Jerusalem as king

21 As they approached Jerusalem and came to Bethphage on the Mount of Olives, Jesus sent two disciples, ²saying to them, "Go to the village ahead of you, and at once you will find a donkey tied there, with her colt by her. Untie them and bring them to me. ³If anyone says anything to you, say that the Lord needs them, and he will send them right away."

⁴This took place to fulfil what was spoken through the prophet:

⁵"Say to Daughter Zion,
   'See, your king comes to you,
gentle and riding on a donkey,
   and on a colt, the foal of a donkey.' "ᵃ

⁶The disciples went and did as Jesus had instructed them. ⁷They brought the donkey and the colt and placed their cloaks on them for Jesus to sit on. ⁸A very large crowd spread their cloaks on the road, while others cut branches from the trees and spread them on the road. ⁹The crowds that went ahead of him and those that followed shouted,

---

a 5 Zech. 9:9

"Hosanna[b] to the Son of David!"

"Blessed is he who comes in the name of the Lord!"[c]

"Hosanna[d] in the highest heaven!"

[10]When Jesus entered Jerusalem, the whole city was stirred and asked, "Who is this?"

[11]The crowds answered, "This is Jesus, the prophet from Nazareth in Galilee."

Jesus at the temple

[12]Jesus entered the temple courts and drove out all who were buying and selling there. He overturned the tables of the money-changers and the benches of those selling doves. [13]"It is written," he said to them, " 'My house will be called a house of prayer,'[e] but you are making it 'a den of robbers.'[f] "

[14]The blind and the lame came to him at the temple, and he healed them. [15]But when the chief priests and the teachers of the law saw the wonderful things he did and the children shouting in the temple courts, "Hosanna to the Son of David," they were indignant.

[16]"Do you hear what these children are saying?" they asked him.

"Yes," replied Jesus, "have you never read,

---

b 9 A Hebrew expression meaning "Save!" which became an exclamation of praise; also in verse 15
c 9 Psalm 118:25,26
d 9 A Hebrew expression meaning "Save!" which became an exclamation of praise; also in verse 15
e 13 Isaiah 56:7
f 13 Jer. 7:11

" 'From the lips of children and infants
  you have ordained praise'[g] ?"

[17]And he left them and went out of the city to Bethany,
where he spent the night.

Jesus curses a fig-tree

[18]Early in the morning, as he was on his way back to the
city, he was hungry. [19]Seeing a fig-tree by the road, he went up
to it but found nothing on it except leaves. Then he said to it,
"May you never bear fruit again!" Immediately the tree withered.

[20]When the disciples saw this, they were amazed. "How did
the fig-tree wither so quickly?" they asked.

[21]Jesus replied, "Truly I tell you, if you have faith and do not
doubt, not only can you do what was done to the fig-tree, but
also you can say to this mountain, 'Go, throw yourself into the
sea,' and it will be done. [22]If you believe, you will receive
whatever you ask for in prayer."

The authority of Jesus questioned

[23]Jesus entered the temple courts, and, while he was teach-
ing, the chief priests and the elders of the people came to him.
"By what authority are you doing these things?" they asked.
"And who gave you this authority?"

[24]Jesus replied, "I will also ask you one question. If you
answer me, I will tell you by what authority I am doing these
things. [25]John's baptism—where did it come from? Was it
from heaven, or of human origin?"

They discussed it among themselves and said, "If we say,

---

g 16 Psalm 8:2 (see Septuagint)

'From heaven', he will ask, 'Then why didn't you believe him?'
²⁶But if we say, 'Of human origin'—we are afraid of the people,
for they all hold that John was a prophet."

²⁷So they answered Jesus, "We don't know."

Then he said, "Neither will I tell you by what authority I am
doing these things.

The parable of the two sons

²⁸"What do you think? There was a man who had two sons.
He went to the first and said, 'Son, go and work today in the
vineyard.'

²⁹" 'I will not,' he answered, but later he changed his mind
and went.

³⁰"Then the father went to the other son and said the same
thing. He answered, 'I will, sir,' but he did not go.

³¹"Which of the two did what his father wanted?"

"The first," they answered.

Jesus said to them, "Truly I tell you, the tax collectors and
the prostitutes are entering the kingdom of God ahead of you.
³²For John came to you to show you the way of righteousness,
and you did not believe him, but the tax collectors and the
prostitutes did. And even after you saw this, you did not
repent and believe him.

The parable of the tenants

³³"Listen to another parable: There was a landowner who
planted a vineyard. He put a wall round it, dug a winepress in
it and built a watchtower. Then he rented the vineyard to
some farmers and moved to another place. ³⁴When the harvest time approached, he sent his servants to the tenants to
collect his fruit.

³⁵"The tenants seized his servants; they beat one, killed

another, and stoned a third. ³⁶Then he sent other servants to them, more than the first time, and the tenants treated them in the same way. ³⁷Last of all, he sent his son to them. 'They will respect my son,' he said.

³⁸"But when the tenants saw the son, they said to each other, 'This is the heir. Come, let's kill him and take his inheritance.' ³⁹So they took him and threw him out of the vineyard and killed him.

⁴⁰"Therefore, when the owner of the vineyard comes, what will he do to those tenants?"

⁴¹"He will bring those wretches to a wretched end," they replied, "and he will rent the vineyard to other tenants, who will give him his share of the crop at harvest time."

⁴²Jesus said to them, "Have you never read in the Scriptures:

" 'The stone the builders rejected
    has become the cornerstone;
  the Lord has done this,
    and it is marvellous in our eyes'ʰ?

⁴³"Therefore I tell you that the kingdom of God will be taken away from you and given to a people who will produce its fruit. ⁴⁴Anyone who falls on this stone will be broken to pieces, but anyone on whom it falls will be crushed."ⁱ

⁴⁵When the chief priests and the Pharisees heard Jesus' parables, they knew he was talking about them. ⁴⁶They looked for a way to arrest him, but they were afraid of the crowd because the people held that he was a prophet.

---

h 42 Psalm 118:22,23
i 44 Some manuscripts do not have verse 44.

The parable of the wedding banquet

22 Jesus spoke to them again in parables, saying: [2]"The kingdom of heaven is like a king who prepared a wedding banquet for his son. [3]He sent his servants to those who had been invited to the banquet to tell them to come, but they refused to come.

[4]"Then he sent some more servants and said, 'Tell those who have been invited that I have prepared my dinner: My oxen and fattened cattle have been slaughtered, and everything is ready. Come to the wedding banquet.'

[5]"But they paid no attention and went off—one to his field, another to his business. [6]The rest seized his servants, ill-treated them and killed them. [7]The king was enraged. He sent his army and destroyed those murderers and burned their city.

[8]"Then he said to his servants, 'The wedding banquet is ready, but those I invited did not deserve to come. [9]Go to the street corners and invite to the banquet anyone you find.' [10]So the servants went out into the streets and gathered all the people they could find, the bad as well as the good, and the wedding hall was filled with guests.

[11]"But when the king came in to see the guests, he noticed a man there who was not wearing wedding clothes. [12]'Friend,' he asked, 'how did you get in here without wedding clothes?' The man was speechless.

[13]"Then the king told the attendants, 'Tie him hand and foot, and throw him outside, into the darkness, where there will be weeping and gnashing of teeth.'

[14]"For many are invited, but few are chosen."

Paying the imperial tax to Caesar

[15]Then the Pharisees went out and laid plans to trap him in his words. [16]They sent their disciples to him along with the

Herodians. "Teacher," they said, "we know that you are a man of integrity and that you teach the way of God in accordance with the truth. You aren't swayed by others, because you pay no attention to who they are. [17]Tell us then, what is your opinion? Is it right to pay the imperial tax[a] to Caesar or not?"

[18]But Jesus, knowing their evil intent, said, "You hypocrites, why are you trying to trap me? [19]Show me the coin used for paying the tax." They brought him a denarius, [20]and he asked them, "Whose likeness is this? And whose inscription?"

[21]"Caesar's," they replied.

Then he said to them, "Give back to Caesar what is Caesar's, and to God what is God's."

[22]When they heard this, they were amazed. So they left him and went away.

Marriage at the resurrection

[23]That same day the Sadducees, who say there is no resurrection, came to him with a question. [24]"Teacher," they said, "Moses told us that if a man dies without having children, his brother must marry the widow and raise up offspring for him. [25]Now there were seven brothers among us. The first one married and died, and since he had no children, he left his wife to his brother. [26]The same thing happened to the second and third brother, right on down to the seventh. [27]Finally, the woman died. [28]Now then, at the resurrection, whose wife will she be of the seven, since all of them were married to her?"

[29]Jesus replied, "You are in error because you do not know the Scriptures or the power of God. [30]At the resurrection people will neither marry nor be given in marriage; they will be like the angels in heaven. [31]But about the resurrection of

---

a 17 A special tax levied on subject peoples, not on Roman citizens

the dead—have you not read what God said to you, [32]'I am the God of Abraham, the God of Isaac, and the God of Jacob'[b]? He is not the God of the dead but of the living."

[33]When the crowds heard this, they were astonished at his teaching.

The greatest commandment

[34]Hearing that Jesus had silenced the Sadducees, the Pharisees got together. [35]One of them, an expert in the law, tested him with this question: [36]"Teacher, which is the greatest commandment in the Law?"

[37]Jesus replied: " 'Love the Lord your God with all your heart and with all your soul and with all your mind.'[c] [38]This is the first and greatest commandment. [39]And the second is like it: 'Love your neighbour as yourself.'[d] [40]All the Law and the Prophets hang on these two commandments."

Whose son is the Messiah?

[41]While the Pharisees were gathered together, Jesus asked them, [42]"What do you think about the Messiah? Whose son is he?"

"The son of David," they replied.

[43]He said to them, "How is it then that David, speaking by the Spirit, calls him 'Lord'? For he says,

[44]" 'The Lord said to my Lord:
   "Sit at my right hand
   until I put your enemies
     under your feet." '[e]

b 32 Exodus 3:6
c 37 Deut. 6:5
d 39 Lev. 19:18
e 44 Psalm 110:1

⁴⁵If then David calls him 'Lord', how can he be his son?" ⁴⁶No-one could say a word in reply, and from that day on no-one dared to ask him any more questions.

A warning against hypocrisy

23 Then Jesus said to the crowds and to his disciples: ²"The teachers of the law and the Pharisees sit in Moses' seat. ³So you must be careful to do everything they tell you. But do not do what they do, for they do not practise what they preach. ⁴They tie up heavy, cumbersome loads and put them on other people's shoulders, but they themselves are not willing to lift a finger to move them.

⁵"Everything they do is done for people to see: They make their phylacteries[a] wide and the tassels on their garments long; ⁶they love the place of honour at banquets and the most important seats in the synagogues; ⁷they love to be greeted with respect in the market-places and to have people call them 'Rabbi'.

⁸"But you are not to be called 'Rabbi', for you have only one Master and you are all brothers. ⁹And do not call anyone on earth 'father', for you have one Father, and he is in heaven. ¹⁰Nor are you to be called 'teacher', for you have one Teacher, the Messiah. ¹¹The greatest among you will be your servant. ¹²For those who exalt themselves will be humbled, and those who humble themselves will be exalted.

Seven woes on the teachers of the law and the Pharisees

¹³ [14]"Woe to you, teachers of the law and Pharisees, you hypocrites! You shut the door of the kingdom of heaven in

---

a 5 That is, boxes containing Scripture verses, worn on forehead and arm

people's faces. You yourselves do not enter, nor will you let those enter who are trying to.

[15]"Woe to you, teachers of the law and Pharisees, you hypocrites! You travel over land and sea to win a single convert, then you make that convert twice as much a child of hell as you are.

[16]"Woe to you, blind guides! You say, 'If anyone swears by the temple, it means nothing; but whoever swears by the gold of the temple is bound by the oath.' [17]You blind fools! Which is greater: the gold, or the temple that makes the gold sacred? [18]You also say, 'If anyone swears by the altar, it means nothing; but whoever swears by the gift on the altar is bound by the oath.' [19]You blind men! Which is greater: the gift, or the altar that makes the gift sacred? [20]Therefore, anyone who swears by the altar swears by it and by everything on it. [21]And anyone who swears by the temple swears by it and by the one who dwells in it. [22]And anyone who swears by heaven swears by God's throne and by the one who sits on it.

[23]"Woe to you, teachers of the law and Pharisees, you hypocrites! You give a tenth of your spices—mint, dill and cumin. But you have neglected the more important matters of the law—justice, mercy and faithfulness. You should have practised the latter, without neglecting the former. [24]You blind guides! You strain out a gnat but swallow a camel.

[25]"Woe to you, teachers of the law and Pharisees, you hypocrites! You clean the outside of the cup and dish, but inside they are full of greed and self-indulgence. [26]Blind Pharisee! First clean the inside of the cup and dish, and then the outside also will be clean.

[27]"Woe to you, teachers of the law and Pharisees, you hypocrites! You are like whitewashed tombs, which look

beautiful on the outside but on the inside are full of the bones of the dead and everything unclean. [28]In the same way, on the outside you appear to people as righteous but on the inside you are full of hypocrisy and wickedness.

[29]"Woe to you, teachers of the law and Pharisees, you hypocrites! You build tombs for the prophets and decorate the graves of the righteous. [30]And you say, 'If we had lived in the days of our ancestors, we would not have taken part with them in shedding the blood of the prophets.' [31]So you testify against yourselves that you are the descendants of those who murdered the prophets. [32]Fill up, then, the measure of the sin of your ancestors!

[33]"You snakes! You brood of vipers! How will you escape being condemned to hell? [34]Therefore I am sending you prophets and sages and teachers. Some of them you will kill and crucify; others you will flog in your synagogues and pursue from town to town. [35]And so on you will come all the righteous blood that has been shed on earth, from the blood of righteous Abel to the blood of Zechariah son of Berekiah, whom you murdered between the temple and the altar. [36]Truly I tell you, all this will come on this generation.

[37]"Jerusalem, Jerusalem, you who kill the prophets and stone those sent to you, how often I have longed to gather your children together, as a hen gathers her chicks under her wings, and you were not willing. [38]Look, your house is left to you desolate. [39]For I tell you, you will not see me again until you say, 'Blessed is he who comes in the name of the Lord.'[b] "

---

b 39 Psalm 118:26

The destruction of the temple and signs of the end times

24 Jesus left the temple and was walking away when his disciples came up to him to call his attention to its buildings. ²"Do you see all these things?" he asked. "Truly I tell you, not one stone here will be left on another; every one will be thrown down."

³As Jesus was sitting on the Mount of Olives, the disciples came to him privately. "Tell us," they said, "when will this happen, and what will be the sign of your coming and of the end of the age?"

⁴Jesus answered: "Watch out that no-one deceives you. ⁵For many will come in my name, claiming, 'I am the Messiah,' and will deceive many. ⁶You will hear of wars and rumours of wars, but see to it that you are not alarmed. Such things must happen, but the end is still to come. ⁷Nation will rise against nation, and kingdom against kingdom. There will be famines and earthquakes in various places. ⁸All these are the beginning of birth-pains.

⁹"Then you will be handed over to be persecuted and put to death, and you will be hated by all nations because of me. ¹⁰At that time many will turn away from the faith and will betray and hate each other, ¹¹and many false prophets will appear and deceive many people. ¹²Because of the increase of wickedness, the love of most will grow cold, ¹³but whoever stands firm to the end will be saved. ¹⁴And this gospel of the kingdom will be preached in the whole world as a testimony to all nations, and then the end will come.

¹⁵"So when you see standing in the holy place 'the abomination that causes desolation,'^a spoken of through the

---

a 15 Daniel 9:27; 11:31; 12:11

prophet Daniel—let the reader understand—[16]then let those who are in Judea flee to the mountains. [17]Let no-one on the housetop go down to take anything out of the house. [18]Let no-one in the field go back to get their cloak. [19]How dreadful it will be in those days for pregnant women and nursing mothers! [20]Pray that your flight will not take place in winter or on the Sabbath. [21]For then there will be great distress, unequalled from the beginning of the world until now—and never to be equalled again.

[22]"If those days had not been cut short, no-one would survive, but for the sake of the elect those days will be shortened. [23]At that time if anyone says to you, 'Look, here is the Messiah!' or, 'There he is!' do not believe it. [24]For false messiahs and false prophets will appear and perform great signs and wonders to deceive, if possible, even the elect. [25]See, I have told you in advance.

[26]"So if anyone tells you, 'There he is, out in the wilderness,' do not go out; or, 'Here he is, in the inner rooms,' do not believe it. [27]For as lightning that comes from the east is visible even in the west, so will be the coming of the Son of Man. [28]Wherever there is a carcass, there the vultures will gather.

[29]"Immediately after the distress of those days

" 'the sun will be darkened,
    and the moon will not give its light;
the stars will fall from the sky,
    and the heavenly bodies will be shaken.'[b]

[30]"At that time the sign of the Son of Man will appear in the sky, and all the peoples of the earth[c] will mourn. They will see

---

b 29 Isaiah 13:10; 34:4
c 30 Or *the tribes of the land*

the Son of Man coming on the clouds of heaven, with power and great glory. [31]And he will send his angels with a loud trumpet call, and they will gather his elect from the four winds, from one end of the heavens to the other.

[32]"Now learn this lesson from the fig-tree: As soon as its twigs become tender and its leaves come out, you know that summer is near. [33]Even so, when you see all these things, you know that it[d] is near, right at the door. [34]Truly I tell you, this generation will certainly not pass away until all these things have happened. [35]Heaven and earth will pass away, but my words will never pass away.

The day and hour unknown

[36]"But about that day or hour no-one knows, not even the angels in heaven, nor the Son,[e] but only the Father. [37]As it was in the days of Noah, so it will be at the coming of the Son of Man. [38]For in the days before the flood, people were eating and drinking, marrying and giving in marriage, up to the day Noah entered the ark; [39]and they knew nothing about what would happen until the flood came and took them all away. That is how it will be at the coming of the Son of Man. [40]Two men will be in the field; one will be taken and the other left. [41]Two women will be grinding with a hand mill; one will be taken and the other left.

[42]"Therefore keep watch, because you do not know on what day your Lord will come. [43]But understand this: If the owner of the house had known at what time of night the thief was coming, he would have kept watch and would not have let his house be broken into. [44]So you also must be ready, because the Son of Man will come at an hour when you do not expect him.

---

d 33 Or *he*
e 36 Some manuscripts do not have *nor the Son.*

⁴⁵"Who then is the faithful and wise servant, whom the master has put in charge of the servants in his household to give them their food at the proper time? ⁴⁶It will be good for that servant whose master finds him doing so when he returns. ⁴⁷Truly I tell you, he will put him in charge of all his possessions. ⁴⁸But suppose that servant is wicked and says to himself, 'My master is staying away a long time,' ⁴⁹and he then begins to beat his fellow-servants and to eat and drink with drunkards. ⁵⁰The master of that servant will come on a day when he does not expect him and at an hour he is not aware of. ⁵¹He will cut him to pieces and assign him a place with the hypocrites, where there will be weeping and gnashing of teeth.

The parable of the ten virgins

25 "At that time the kingdom of heaven will be like ten virgins who took their lamps and went out to meet the bridegroom. ²Five of them were foolish and five were wise. ³The foolish ones took their lamps but did not take any oil with them. ⁴The wise, however, took oil in jars along with their lamps. ⁵The bridegroom was a long time in coming, and they all became drowsy and fell asleep.

⁶"At midnight the cry rang out: 'Here's the bridegroom! Come out to meet him!'

⁷"Then all the virgins woke up and trimmed their lamps. ⁸The foolish ones said to the wise, 'Give us some of your oil; our lamps are going out.'

⁹" 'No,' they replied, 'there may not be enough for both us and you. Instead, go to those who sell oil and buy some for yourselves.'

¹⁰"But while they were on their way to buy the oil, the bridegroom arrived. The virgins who were ready went in

with him to the wedding banquet. And the door was shut.

¹¹"Later the others also came. 'Sir! Sir!' they said. 'Open the door for us!'

¹²"But he replied, 'Truly I tell you, I don't know you.'

¹³"Therefore keep watch, because you do not know the day or the hour.

The parable of the bags of gold

¹⁴"Again, it will be like a man going on a journey, who called his servants and entrusted his wealth to them. ¹⁵To one he gave five bags of gold, to another two bags, and to another one bag,[a] each according to his ability. Then he went on his journey. ¹⁶The man who had received five bags of gold went at once and put his money to work and gained five bags more. ¹⁷So also, the one with two bags of gold gained two more. ¹⁸But the man who had received one bag went off, dug a hole in the ground and hid his master's money.

¹⁹"After a long time the master of those servants returned and settled accounts with them. ²⁰The man who had received five bags of gold brought the other five. 'Master,' he said, 'you entrusted me with five bags of gold. See, I have gained five more.'

²¹"His master replied, 'Well done, good and faithful servant! You have been faithful with a few things; I will put you in charge of many things. Come and share your master's happiness!'

²²"The man with two bags of gold also came. 'Master,' he said, 'you entrusted me with two bags of gold: see, I have gained two more.'

---

a 15 Greek *five talents . . . two talents . . . one talent*; also throughout this parable; a talent was worth about 20 years of a day labourer's wage.

²³"His master replied, 'Well done, good and faithful servant! You have been faithful with a few things; I will put you in charge of many things. Come and share your master's happiness!'

²⁴"Then the man who had received one bag of gold came. 'Master,' he said, 'I knew that you are a hard man, harvesting where you have not sown and gathering where you have not scattered seed. ²⁵So I was afraid and went out and hid your gold in the ground. See, here is what belongs to you.'

²⁶"His master replied, 'You wicked, lazy servant! So you knew that I harvest where I have not sown and gather where I have not scattered seed? ²⁷Well then, you should have put my money on deposit with the bankers, so that when I returned I would have received it back with interest.

²⁸" 'Take the bag of gold from him and give it to the one who has ten bags. ²⁹For those who have will be given more, and they will have an abundance. As for those who do not have, even what they have will be taken from them. ³⁰And throw that worthless servant outside, into the darkness, where there will be weeping and gnashing of teeth.'

The sheep and the goats

³¹"When the Son of Man comes in his glory, and all the angels with him, he will sit on his glorious throne. ³²All the nations will be gathered before him, and he will separate the people one from another as a shepherd separates the sheep from the goats. ³³He will put the sheep on his right and the goats on his left.

³⁴"Then the King will say to those on his right, 'Come, you who are blessed by my Father; take your inheritance, the kingdom prepared for you since the creation of the world. ³⁵For I was hungry and you gave me something to eat, I was

thirsty and you gave me something to drink, I was a stranger and you invited me in, [36]I needed clothes and you clothed me, I was ill and you looked after me, I was in prison and you came to visit me.'

[37]"Then the righteous will answer him, 'Lord, when did we see you hungry and feed you, or thirsty and give you something to drink? [38]When did we see you a stranger and invite you in, or needing clothes and clothe you? [39]When did we see you ill or in prison and go to visit you?'

[40]"The King will reply, 'Truly I tell you, whatever you did for one of the least of these brothers and sisters of mine, you did for me.'

[41]"Then he will say to those on his left, 'Depart from me, you who are cursed, into the eternal fire prepared for the devil and his angels. [42]For I was hungry and you gave me nothing to eat, I was thirsty and you gave me nothing to drink, [43]I was a stranger and you did not invite me in, I needed clothes and you did not clothe me, I was ill and in prison and you did not look after me.'

[44]"They also will answer, 'Lord, when did we see you hungry or thirsty or a stranger or needing clothes or ill or in prison, and did not help you?'

[45]"He will reply, 'Truly I tell you, whatever you did not do for one of the least of these, you did not do for me.'

[46]"Then they will go away to eternal punishment, but the righteous to eternal life."

The plot against Jesus

26 When Jesus had finished saying all these things, he said to his disciples, [2]"As you know, the Passover is two days away—and the Son of Man will be handed over to be crucified."

³Then the chief priests and the elders of the people assembled in the palace of the high priest, whose name was Caiaphas, ⁴and they plotted to arrest Jesus in some sly way and kill him. ⁵"But not during the Festival," they said, "or there may be a riot among the people."

Jesus anointed at Bethany

⁶While Jesus was in Bethany in the home of Simon the Leper, ⁷a woman came to him with an alabaster jar of very expensive perfume, which she poured on his head as he was reclining at the table.

⁸When the disciples saw this, they were indignant. "Why this waste?" they asked. ⁹"This perfume could have been sold at a high price and the money given to the poor."

¹⁰Aware of this, Jesus said to them, "Why are you bothering this woman? She has done a beautiful thing to me. ¹¹The poor you will always have with you,ᵃ but you will not always have me. ¹²When she poured this perfume on my body, she did it to prepare me for burial. ¹³Truly I tell you, wherever this gospel is preached throughout the world, what she has done will also be told, in memory of her."

Judas agrees to betray Jesus

¹⁴Then one of the Twelve—the one called Judas Iscariot—went to the chief priests ¹⁵and asked, "What are you willing to give me if I deliver him over to you?" So they counted out for him thirty pieces of silver. ¹⁶From then on Judas watched for an opportunity to hand him over.

---

a 11 See Deut. 15:11.

The Lord's Supper

¹⁷On the first day of the Festival of Unleavened Bread, the disciples came to Jesus and asked, "Where do you want us to make preparations for you to eat the Passover?"

¹⁸He replied, "Go into the city to a certain man and tell him, 'The Teacher says: My appointed time is near. I am going to celebrate the Passover with my disciples at your house.' " ¹⁹So the disciples did as Jesus had directed them and prepared the Passover.

²⁰When evening came, Jesus was reclining at the table with the Twelve. ²¹And while they were eating, he said, "Truly I tell you, one of you will betray me."

²²They were very sad and began to say to him one after the other, "Surely not I, Lord?"

²³Jesus replied, "The one who has dipped his hand into the bowl with me will betray me. ²⁴The Son of Man will go just as it is written about him. But woe to that man who betrays the Son of Man! It would be better for him if he had not been born."

²⁵Then Judas, the one who would betray him, said, "Surely not I, Rabbi?"

Jesus answered, "You have said so."

²⁶While they were eating, Jesus took bread, and when he had given thanks, he broke it and gave it to his disciples, saying, "Take and eat; this is my body."

²⁷Then he took the cup, and when he had given thanks, he gave it to them, saying, "Drink from it, all of you. ²⁸This is my blood of the^b covenant, which is poured out for many for the forgiveness of sins. ²⁹I tell you, I will not drink of this fruit of

---

b 28 Some manuscripts *the new*

the vine from now on until that day when I drink it new with you in my Father's kingdom."

³⁰When they had sung a hymn, they went out to the Mount of Olives.

Jesus predicts Peter's denial

³¹Then Jesus told them, "This very night you will all fall away on account of me, for it is written:

" 'I will strike the shepherd,
   and the sheep of the flock will be scattered.'^c
³²But after I have risen, I will go ahead of you into Galilee."

³³Peter replied, "Even if all fall away on account of you, I never will."

³⁴"Truly I tell you," Jesus answered, "this very night, before the cock crows, you will disown me three times."

³⁵But Peter declared, "Even if I have to die with you, I will never disown you." And all the other disciples said the same.

Gethsemane

³⁶Then Jesus went with his disciples to a place called Gethsemane, and he said to them, "Sit here while I go over there and pray." ³⁷He took Peter and the two sons of Zebedee along with him, and he began to be sorrowful and troubled. ³⁸Then he said to them, "My soul is overwhelmed with sorrow to the point of death. Stay here and keep watch with me."

³⁹Going a little farther, he fell with his face to the ground and prayed, "My Father, if it is possible, may this cup be taken from me. Yet not as I will, but as you will."

⁴⁰Then he returned to his disciples and found them sleeping. "Couldn't you men keep watch with me for one hour?" he

---

c 31 Zech. 13:7

asked Peter. [41]"Watch and pray so that you will not fall into temptation. The spirit is willing, but the flesh is weak."

[42]He went away a second time and prayed, "My Father, if it is not possible for this cup to be taken away unless I drink it, may your will be done."

[43]When he came back, he again found them sleeping, because their eyes were heavy. [44]So he left them and went away once more and prayed the third time, saying the same thing.

[45]Then he returned to the disciples and said to them, "Are you still sleeping and resting? Look, the hour is near, and the Son of Man is delivered into the hands of sinners. [46]Rise! Let us go! Here comes my betrayer!"

Jesus arrested

[47]While he was still speaking, Judas, one of the Twelve, arrived. With him was a large crowd armed with swords and clubs, sent from the chief priests and the elders of the people. [48]Now the betrayer had arranged a signal with them: "The one I kiss is the man; arrest him." [49]Going at once to Jesus, Judas said, "Greetings, Rabbi!" and kissed him.

[50]Jesus replied, "Friend, do what you came for."[d]

Then the men stepped forward, seized Jesus and arrested him. [51]With that, one of Jesus' companions reached for his sword, drew it out and struck the servant of the high priest, cutting off his ear.

[52]"Put your sword back in its place," Jesus said to him, "for all who draw the sword will die by the sword. [53]Do you think I cannot call on my Father, and he will at once put at my disposal more than twelve legions of angels? [54]But how then

d 50 Or *"Friend, why have you come?"*

would the Scriptures be fulfilled that say it must happen in this way?"

⁵⁵In that hour Jesus said to the crowd, "Am I leading a rebellion, that you have come out with swords and clubs to capture me? Every day I sat in the temple courts teaching, and you did not arrest me. ⁵⁶But this has all taken place that the writings of the prophets might be fulfilled." Then all the disciples deserted him and fled.

Jesus before the Sanhedrin

⁵⁷Those who had arrested Jesus took him to Caiaphas the high priest, where the teachers of the law and the elders had assembled. ⁵⁸But Peter followed him at a distance, right up to the courtyard of the high priest. He entered and sat down with the guards to see the outcome.

⁵⁹The chief priests and the whole Sanhedrin were looking for false evidence against Jesus so that they could put him to death. ⁶⁰But they did not find any, though many false witnesses came forward.

Finally two came forward ⁶¹and declared, "This fellow said, 'I am able to destroy the temple of God and rebuild it in three days.' "

⁶²Then the high priest stood up and said to Jesus, "Are you not going to answer? What is this testimony that these men are bringing against you?" ⁶³But Jesus remained silent.

The high priest said to him, "I charge you under oath by the living God: Tell us if you are the Messiah, the Son of God."

⁶⁴"It is as you say," Jesus replied. "But I say to all of you: From now on you will see the Son of Man sitting at the right hand of the Mighty One and coming on the clouds of heaven."[e]

---

e 64 See Psalm 110:1; Daniel 7:13.

⁶⁵Then the high priest tore his clothes and said, "He has spoken blasphemy! Why do we need any more witnesses? Look, now you have heard the blasphemy. ⁶⁶What do you think?"

"He is worthy of death," they answered.

⁶⁷Then they spat in his face and struck him with their fists. Others slapped him ⁶⁸and said, "Prophesy to us, Messiah. Who hit you?"

Peter disowns Jesus

⁶⁹Now Peter was sitting out in the courtyard, and a servant-girl came to him. "You also were with Jesus of Galilee," she said.

⁷⁰But he denied it before them all. "I don't know what you're talking about," he said.

⁷¹Then he went out to the gateway, where another servant-girl saw him and said to the people there, "This fellow was with Jesus of Nazareth."

⁷²He denied it again, with an oath: "I don't know the man!"

⁷³After a little while, those standing there went up to Peter and said, "Surely you are one of them; your accent gives you away."

⁷⁴Then he began to call down curses, and he swore to them, "I don't know the man!"

Immediately a cock crowed. ⁷⁵Then Peter remembered the word Jesus had spoken: "Before the cock crows, you will disown me three times." And he went outside and wept bitterly.

Judas hangs himself

27 Early in the morning, all the chief priests and the elders of the people came to the decision to put Jesus to death. ²They bound him, led him away and handed him over to Pilate, the governor.

³When Judas, who had betrayed him, saw that Jesus was condemned, he was seized with remorse and returned the thirty silver coins to the chief priests and the elders. ⁴"I have sinned," he said, "for I have betrayed innocent blood."

"What is that to us?" they replied. "That's your responsibility."

⁵So Judas threw the money into the temple and left. Then he went away and hanged himself.

⁶The chief priests picked up the coins and said, "It is against the law to put this into the treasury, since it is blood money." ⁷So they decided to use the money to buy the potter's field as a burial place for foreigners. ⁸That is why it has been called the Field of Blood to this day. ⁹Then what was spoken by Jeremiah the prophet was fulfilled: "They took the thirty pieces of silver, the price set on him by the people of Israel, ¹⁰and they used them to buy the potter's field, as the Lord commanded me."ᵃ

Jesus before Pilate

¹¹Meanwhile Jesus stood before the governor, and the governor asked him, "Are you the king of the Jews?"

"You have said so," Jesus replied.

¹²When he was accused by the chief priests and the elders, he gave no answer. ¹³Then Pilate asked him, "Don't you hear the testimony they are bringing against you?" ¹⁴But Jesus made no reply, not even to a single charge—to the great amazement of the governor.

¹⁵Now it was the governor's custom at the Festival to release a prisoner chosen by the crowd. ¹⁶At that time they had a well-known prisoner whose name was Jesusᵇ Barabbas. ¹⁷So when

a 10 See Zech. 11:12,13; Jer. 19:1–13; 32:6–9.
b 16 Many manuscripts do not have *Jesus*.

the crowd had gathered, Pilate asked them, "Which one do you want me to release to you: Jesus[c] Barabbas, or Jesus who is called the Messiah?" [18]For he knew it was out of envy that they had handed Jesus over to him.

[19]While Pilate was sitting on the judge's seat, his wife sent him this message: "Don't have anything to do with that innocent man, for I have suffered a great deal today in a dream because of him."

[20]But the chief priests and the elders persuaded the crowd to ask for Barabbas and to have Jesus executed.

[21]"Which of the two do you want me to release to you?" asked the governor.

"Barabbas," they answered.

[22]"What shall I do, then, with Jesus who is called the Messiah?" Pilate asked.

They all answered, "Crucify him!"

[23]"Why? What crime has he committed?" asked Pilate.

But they shouted all the louder, "Crucify him!"

[24]When Pilate saw that he was getting nowhere, but that instead an uproar was starting, he took water and washed his hands in front of the crowd. "I am innocent of this man's blood," he said. "It is your responsibility!"

[25]All the people answered, "His blood is on us and on our children!"

[26]Then he released Barabbas to them. But he had Jesus flogged, and handed him over to be crucified.

The soldiers mock Jesus

[27]Then the governor's soldiers took Jesus into the Praetorium and gathered the whole company of soldiers round him.

---

c 17 Many manuscripts do not have *Jesus*.

²⁸They stripped him and put a scarlet robe on him, ²⁹and then twisted together a crown of thorns and set it on his head. They put a staff in his right hand as a sceptre. Then they knelt in front of him and mocked him. "Hail, king of the Jews!" they said. ³⁰They spat on him, and took the staff and struck him on the head again and again. ³¹After they had mocked him, they took off the robe and put his own clothes on him. Then they led him away to crucify him.

The crucifixion of Jesus

³²As they were going out, they met a man from Cyrene, named Simon, and they forced him to carry the cross. ³³They came to a place called Golgotha (which means The Place of the Skull). ³⁴There they offered Jesus wine to drink, mixed with gall; but after tasting it, he refused to drink it. ³⁵When they had crucified him, they divided up his clothes by casting lots. ³⁶And sitting down, they kept watch over him there. ³⁷Above his head they placed the written charge against him: THIS IS JESUS, THE KING OF THE JEWS. ³⁸Two rebels were crucified with him, one on his right and one on his left. ³⁹Those who passed by hurled insults at him, shaking their heads ⁴⁰and saying, "You who are going to destroy the temple and build it in three days, save yourself! Come down from the cross, if you are the Son of God!"

⁴¹In the same way the chief priests, the teachers of the law and the elders mocked him. ⁴²"He saved others," they said, "but he can't save himself! He's the king of Israel! Let him come down now from the cross, and we will believe in him. ⁴³He trusts in God. Let God rescue him now if he wants him, for he said, 'I am the Son of God.' " ⁴⁴In the same way the rebels who were crucified with him also heaped insults on him.

The death of Jesus

[45]From noon until three in the afternoon darkness came over all the land. [46]About three in the afternoon Jesus cried out in a loud voice, *"Eli, Eli,*[d] *lema sabachthani?"*—which means, "My God, my God, why have you forsaken me?"[e]

[47]When some of those standing there heard this, they said, "He's calling Elijah."

[48]Immediately one of them ran and got a sponge. He filled it with wine vinegar, put it on a staff, and offered it to Jesus to drink. [49]The rest said, "Now leave him alone. Let's see if Elijah comes to save him."

[50]And when Jesus had cried out again in a loud voice, he gave up his spirit.

[51]At that moment the curtain of the temple was torn in two from top to bottom. The earth shook, the rocks split [52]and the tombs broke open. The bodies of many holy people who had died were raised to life. [53]They came out of the tombs after Jesus' resurrection and[f] went into the holy city and appeared to many people.

[54]When the centurion and those with him who were guarding Jesus saw the earthquake and all that had happened, they were terrified, and exclaimed, "Surely he was the Son of God!"

[55]Many women were there, watching from a distance. They had followed Jesus from Galilee to care for his needs. [56]Among them were Mary Magdalene, Mary the mother of James and Joseph,[g] and the mother of Zebedee's sons.

---

d 46 Some manuscripts *Eloi, Eloi*

e 46 Psalm 22:1

f 53 Or *tombs, and after Jesus' resurrection they*

g 56 Greek *Joses*, a variant of *Joseph*

The burial of Jesus

[57]As evening approached, there came a rich man from Arimathea, named Joseph, who had himself become a disciple of Jesus. [58]Going to Pilate, he asked for Jesus' body, and Pilate ordered that it be given to him. [59]Joseph took the body, wrapped it in a clean linen cloth, [60]and placed it in his own new tomb that he had cut out of the rock. He rolled a big stone in front of the entrance to the tomb and went away. [61]Mary Magdalene and the other Mary were sitting there opposite the tomb.

The guard at the tomb

[62]The next day, the one after Preparation Day, the chief priests and the Pharisees went to Pilate. [63]"Sir," they said, "we remember that while he was still alive that deceiver said, 'After three days I will rise again.' [64]So give the order for the tomb to be made secure until the third day. Otherwise, his disciples may come and steal the body and tell the people that he has been raised from the dead. This last deception will be worse than the first."

[65]"Take a guard," Pilate answered. "Go, make the tomb as secure as you know how." [66]So they went and made the tomb secure by putting a seal on the stone and posting the guard.

Jesus has risen

28 After the Sabbath, at dawn on the first day of the week, Mary Magdalene and the other Mary went to look at the tomb.

[2]There was a violent earthquake, for an angel of the Lord came down from heaven and, going to the tomb, rolled back the stone and sat on it. [3]His appearance was like lightning, and

his clothes were white as snow. [4]The guards were so afraid of him that they shook and became like dead men.

[5]The angel said to the women, "Do not be afraid, for I know that you are looking for Jesus, who was crucified. [6]He is not here; he has risen, just as he said. Come and see the place where he lay. [7]Then go quickly and tell his disciples: 'He has risen from the dead and is going ahead of you into Galilee. There you will see him.' Now I have told you."

[8]So the women hurried away from the tomb, afraid yet filled with joy, and ran to tell his disciples. [9]Suddenly Jesus met them. "Greetings," he said. They came to him, clasped his feet and worshipped him. [10]Then Jesus said to them, "Do not be afraid. Go and tell my brothers to go to Galilee; there they will see me."

The guards' report

[11]While the women were on their way, some of the guards went into the city and reported to the chief priests everything that had happened. [12]When the chief priests had met with the elders and devised a plan, they gave the soldiers a large sum of money, [13]telling them, "You are to say, 'His disciples came during the night and stole him away while we were asleep.' [14]If this report gets to the governor, we will satisfy him and keep you out of trouble." [15]So the soldiers took the money and did as they were instructed. And this story has been widely circulated among the Jews to this very day.

The great commission

[16]Then the eleven disciples went to Galilee, to the mountain where Jesus had told them to go. [17]When they saw him, they worshipped him; but some doubted. [18]Then Jesus came to them and said, "All authority in heaven and on earth has been

given to me. [19]Therefore go and make disciples of all nations, baptising them in[a] the name of the Father and of the Son and of the Holy Spirit, [20]and teaching them to obey everything I have commanded you. And surely I am with you always, to the very end of the age."

---

a 19 Or *into*; see Acts 8:16; 19:5; Romans 6:3; 1 Cor. 1:13; 10:2; Gal. 3:27.